Raising the Bar

The Crucial Role of the Lawyer
in Society

TALMAGE BOSTON

Raising the Bar

The Crucial Role of the Lawyer in Society

5/10/12

To David Elmquist —
A great lawyer & a dear
friend.

Best Wishes,
TAB

Austin 2012

The State Bar of Texas, through its TexasBarBooks Department, publishes practice books prepared and edited by knowledgeable authors to give practicing lawyers as much assistance as possible. The competence of the authors ensures outstanding professional products, but, of course, neither the State Bar of Texas, the editors, nor the authors make either express or implied warranties in regard to their use. Each lawyer must depend on his or her own knowledge of the law and expertise in the use or modification of these materials.

The use of the masculine gender in parts of this book is purely for literary convenience and should, of course, be understood to include the feminine gender as well.

It is not the policy of the State Bar of Texas to assert political positions. It is our hope that this publication fosters healthy discussion about legal issues and the legal profession. Any views expressed in this publication are those of the author and do not necessarily reflect the opinions of the leadership or staff of the Bar.

International Standard Book Number: 978-1-892542-84-7
Library of Congress Control Number: 2011940491

© 2012 State Bar of Texas
Austin, TX 78711

Printed in the United States of America

MIX
Paper from
responsible sources
FSC® C004881

This book is dedicated to
Charles Boston, Austin McCloud, Robert B. Payne,
Lee D. Vendig, and Walter M. Spradley,
the most important legal mentors of my life.

By far the most useful and generally applicable variant of the species, however, is the lawyer. He is the lubricant of society's essential machinery, making sure as far as possible that its parts mesh rather than clash. Or, to vary the metaphor, he is a sort of universal interpreter, making the words of one speaker intelligible to another.

WILLIAM A. RUSHER

Contents

Foreword

My friend Talmage Boston has made a significant contribution to legal lore through his careful recounting of the role of leading lawyers in American life and literature. His observations on the lives and careers of each of the legal giants with whom he deals remind us anew of the centrality to the American Experience of the rule of law and those entrusted with its application.

My own view is understandingly informed by a career-long effort to heed the challenge enunciated by Supreme Court Justice Oliver Wendell Holmes: "It is required of a man that he should share the passion and action of his time, at peril of being judged not to have lived." What a blessing for me to have had the chance to make a difference through addressing important challenges not only as governor of my home state of Pennsylvania but through service to two great presidents, Ronald Reagan and George H. W. Bush, as attorney general of the United States. These opportunities would not have come to me if I had not been—first, last, and always—a practicing lawyer.

In recent years, to be sure, we've seen the reputation of the legal profession decline. That decline probably started with the Watergate crisis, which was the tragic story of a lawyer-president and his support team (made up of "an awful lot of lawyers") who allowed themselves to lose sight of their public duty to uphold the rule of law. We have all paid a price for their failure to honor that most important professional responsibility.

Because of our diminished stature in the public eye, it seems to me that every single lawyer in this great country of ours, starting now, needs to take personal responsibility to "raise the bar" and participate in rebuilding the reputation of our great profession. Talmage Boston reminds us that lawyers over time have played a crucial role in elevating the United States to the position it holds today as preeminent in the world order, and every American citizen needs to be reminded of that fact. If we don't do it, no one else will.

Talmage has done his part to fulfill that responsibility by writing this fine book. We can all use the arguments he has provided us in these pages to remind our fellow citizens, among other things, for example, that our nation's greatest hero of all time, Abraham Lincoln, was a smart, hard-working lawyer. "Honest Abe" couldn't have accomplished all he did as president had he not possessed the superior communication and analytical skills that he first developed as a lawyer.

We also need to jog the public's memory that the greatest hero ever to come out of an American novel or appear in a movie, Atticus Finch, was a courageous lawyer unafraid of representing to the best of his ability an unpopular client in an unpopular case.

And we don't have to go far back in time or enter a fictional realm to find lawyers who made America better and even made the world better. Talmage has fully told the stories of the major historic accomplishments of two of his favorite lawyers, Leon Jaworski and James A. Baker, III, both Texans who made important contributions during our lifetimes.

In recent years, it's been exhilarating to see lawyers enter new arenas in our society and make a difference. Certainly, the world of writing fiction is one of those arenas, so I'm pleased that Talmage has a chapter on lawyer-novelists and how their good work does more than merely entertain us.

Although Theodore Roosevelt has always been one of my personal heroes, this book reminds us of how he butted heads late in his career with Justice Holmes and other legal dignitaries of his era over the importance of the rule of law. This serves to remind us as advocates of our professional responsibility to protect our Constitution from political power grabs—again, if we don't do it, nobody else will.

Finally, regarding Talmage's last chapter, I share his opinion that our main job as lawyers representing clients involved in disputes is to get their problems solved as soon as we can, and as well as we can. If the public understands by our conduct and sense of urgency that we are doing what it takes to get matters handled promptly and successfully, allowing people to get on with their lives, our profession's reputation will be restored that much sooner.

Several years ago, I titled my autobiography *Where the Evidence Leads* (revised paperback edition, University of Pittsburgh Press, 2010), because I saw that my main job as a lawyer in both public and private roles was to always seek the truth, free from personal, political, or partisan considerations. To do that, I've done my best to literally "follow the evidence wherever it leads." America would not be the great country it is, governed by our Constitution and the rule of law for well over two hundred years, if it were not for lawyers willing to do so. That is the truth, and all the evidence of history and insights from my time in government service and private practice has only confirmed that truth.

As Talmage Boston has done in the pages ahead, I challenge all lawyers to "raise the bar," so all in our society can have a deeper appreciation for the vital function served by lawyers both in the past and the present. I encourage readers to take up this book's signal message, supported by these marvelous stories from our history, and use it to become ambassadors for our profession throughout our various social and professional networks.

Last year, as Talmage notes, the State Bar of Texas sponsored a program celebrating the fiftieth anniversary of the publication of Harper Lee's *To Kill a Mockingbird*. My contribution was to suggest that the most pertinent question for any lawyer facing the challenge of making a close call on tough decisions was to ask at the critical moment, "What would Atticus Finch do?" Talmage Boston has greatly expanded the number of additional sources from whence answers might be forthcoming to even the most vexing questions we are likely to encounter in today's practice of law. For this we should all be genuinely grateful.

Dick Thornburgh
Washington, DC
August 1, 2011

Raising the Bar

The Crucial Role of the Lawyer
in Society

Introduction

On the occasion of Abraham Lincoln's two-hundredth birthday, February 12, 2009, Pulitzer Prize–winning historian James McPherson spoke at a luncheon in Dallas sponsored by the State Bar of Texas about his latest book, *Tried by War: Abraham Lincoln as Commander-in-Chief* (New York: Penguin, 2008), which addressed President Lincoln's stellar performance as commander in chief during the Civil War. After Dr. McPherson finished his speech, I asked him, "Do you believe Abraham Lincoln could have achieved his many political and military successes throughout his presidency if he had not been a consummate lawyer?"

The reigning dean of American Civil War historians, mindful of the many ways Lincoln repeatedly invoked his war powers in a manner that tested but withstood constitutional scrutiny, gave a quick, succinct answer: "No. His being a lawyer was essential to his accomplishments as president."

Sixteen months after that luncheon, at its 2010 annual meeting, the State Bar of Texas celebrated the golden anniversary of Harper Lee's classic novel, *To Kill a Mockingbird*, by scheduling a full day of programs devoted to exploring the impact of Atticus Finch. Speakers for the occasion included former Pennsylvania governor

---

Facing page: Gregory Peck as Atticus Finch in the movie *To Kill a Mockingbird*. Photo by Silver Screen Collection. Photo courtesy of Getty Images.

and U.S. attorney general Dick Thornburgh; esteemed U.S. district judge W. Royal Furgeson Jr.; current Baylor University president and former solicitor general Ken Starr; legendary Houston trial lawyer and author of *I Remember Atticus* (Austin: TexasBarBooks, 2004) Jim Perdue; former ABA and State Bar Litigation Section chair Kim Askew; my friend Bill Parrish, a fine IP litigator and *Mockingbird*'s ultimate aficionado; and me. Lawyers and judges from all over Texas packed each session, hour after hour, seemingly incapable of getting enough information about the lawyer who became our profession's greatest fictional hero.

This confluence of Abraham Lincoln and Atticus Finch in 2009–2010, and the state bar's recognizing them as the ultimate role models for lawyers, created the inspiration for this book. Not co-incidentally, that same meshing of legal giants had occurred in my life many decades before, and it drove my decision at a young age to become a lawyer. Harper Lee opened *To Kill a Mockingbird* with nineteenth-century British writer Charles Lamb's astute observation: "Lawyers, I suppose, were children once," and before reaching the age of ten, I took those words to heart.

During my grade school years in the first half of the 1960s, simultaneous with the rise of the American civil rights movement, our country acknowledged the centennial of the Civil War with an outpouring of history books, television documentaries, and even children's trading cards devoted to the events of 1861 to 1865. In the big middle of the war's observance was its greatest hero—the tall, bearded guy in the stovepipe hat, whose public statements flowed with the eloquence of Shakespeare and the King James Bible, due largely to the fact (as I learned many years later) that throughout his life he had memorized large chunks of Shakespeare and the King James Bible. Digging into the Lincoln biographies in our school library caused me to recognize that before becoming president, Father Abraham had honed the skills that fueled his political achievements by spending his pre–White House years as a trial and appellate lawyer.

At the same time my young soul became immersed in all things Lincoln, in early 1963, my parents took me to see the movie *To Kill a Mockingbird*, featuring Gregory Peck in his Academy Award–

winning portrayal of Atticus Finch. Right there on the silver screen, before my very eyes, appeared a character as wise, courageous, and eloquent as Abraham Lincoln. And by golly, just like Honest Abe, Mr. Finch was a trial lawyer, too!

With those images imbedded in my mind, and Messrs. Lincoln and Finch secure as the top non–Major League Baseball player heroes of my childhood, there clearly was only one thing a nine-and-a-half-year-old boy growing up in Houston, Texas, during the mid-1960s, who possessed only meager baseball skills, could realistically aspire to be when he grew up—a lawyer! So at that tender age, I hitched my career dream wagon to the star "aurora lawyerealis," and over the next fifteen years I turned that dream into a reality, culminating with graduating from law school and passing the bar exam in 1978.

Fast-forward a few decades, and, lo and behold, this not-always-humble scrivener has now been a practicing lawyer over thirty years—ample time to have had many inspirations, seen many changes (some good, some bad), and formed many opinions about my chosen profession.

As developed in the upcoming chapters, my conclusions are the following:

- If today's lawyers recommit to being guided in our daily practice by the examples of Abraham Lincoln and Atticus Finch, then the public's perception of our essential role as society's problem solvers and the lubricant of its human machinery can be restored.

- At the top of the mountain in the modern era, two lawyers, Leon Jaworski and James A. Baker, III (coincidentally both from Texas), deserve special attention in the ways they expanded our profession's positive impact by fully utilizing their consummate professional skills—Colonel Jaworski as litigator and Secretary Baker as counselor and diplomat—to solve major problems that threatened the stability of American society and our world.

- Lawyer-novelists Louis Auchincloss, Richard North Patterson, and John Grisham have expanded the profession's impact by addressing contemporary social, legal, and political issues in their best-selling books. And because of the way these men's work has been necessarily shaped by their legal experiences, they have succeeded in expanding public consciousness to new and deeper perspectives on their subjects.

- Theodore Roosevelt's unique life provides direction to today's profession, teaching that (1) pursuing one's passions in life's arena nonstop for several decades at a frenzied pace produces a train wreck of the heart, mind, body, and soul; and (2) lawyers must stay ever vigilant in protecting the rule of law and an independent judiciary in the face of political demagoguery.

- Finally, in an increasingly complex world where conflicts are ever present, enhanced discovery tools and dispute-resolution alternatives are a good thing, the partisan political election of judges is a bad thing (because it results too often in under-qualified and sometimes corrupt judges presiding over trials and appeals), and therefore the vanishing trial is not a bad thing.

Rome wasn't built in a day. Every long journey begins with a single step. Lawyers must now step up, raise the bar, and bring the profession back to its once-hallowed place in our society—the place where a young Abraham Lincoln said to himself in his mid-twenties, and Leon Jaworski said to himself in his teens, "Out of all the career opportunities potentially available to me, I want to be a lawyer!"; where a young Harper Lee said to herself in her late twenties, "Out of all the subjects on which I could write, I want to create a novel about a courageous and wise hero who's a lawyer—just like my father!"; and where James A. Baker, III, looked in awe and respect on his great-grandfather, grandfather, and father as prominent attorneys and aspired to grow up and be just like them.

Yes, being a lawyer once held such a place in the American mind-set. And if we don't find a way to remind ourselves and those who aren't lawyers of the profession's immense contribution to our rich history, national skill set, problem-solving machinery, and integral role in preserving the rule of law, then we will have no one to blame but ourselves.

CHAPTER ONE

The Timeless Inspiration of Abraham Lincoln and Atticus Finch

Beethoven's music will never go out of style. Dostoevsky's prose will never fail to captivate. Rembrandt's paintings will never lose their masterpiece status. Yes, there are an elite few in the various human endeavors whose work is so superior that any ill-considered criticism directed at them in any era has as much chance of diminishing their stature as an ocean wave has of making a dent in a shoreline boulder.

For the species of *Homo sapiens* known as "lawyers," the two men at the top of the profession's mountain are Abraham Lincoln and Atticus Finch. Their names are synonymous with high integrity, penetrating empathy, zealous advocacy, profound wisdom, and unwavering self-control.

They both were lawyer-politicians, managing to practice law while serving in the legislature. They even looked alike. Historian Brian Dirck, in his book *Lincoln the Lawyer*, noted their physical similarity

---

Facing page: Abraham Lincoln. Photo courtesy of the Library of Congress.

when he pointed out that when Norman Rockwell decided to paint *Mr. Lincoln for the Defense* in 1962, two years after the publication of *To Kill a Mockingbird*, he chose to have his subject resemble "an antebellum Atticus Finch, standing in the courtroom with tie and suspenders askew, planting his brawny forearm and fist on a nearby table,"[1] with his glasses in hand and beads of sweat on his shining forehead.

Not coincidentally, how Mr. Rockwell envisioned Abraham Lincoln the lawyer matched the way Harper Lee described Atticus Finch during his closing argument at Tom Robinson's trial, when the narrator, Scout, described Atticus as having surprisingly unbuttoned his vest and collar, loosened his tie, removed his coat, and begun to sweat.

For those with a hazy memory about the particulars of exactly what it is that gives this esteemed duo their monumental stature, this chapter attempts to adjust the lens and bring Messrs. Lincoln and Finch back into focus as living, breathing lawyers who performed at the highest professional level in a way that will never go out of style and will always be worthy of imitation.

ABRAHAM LINCOLN

Having grown up in bona fide poverty, Abraham Lincoln qualified as a poster child for what French historian Alexis de Tocqueville saw in the 1830s as the essence of the American spirit—that people of the United States had a "longing to rise" to higher stations in life and "a thirst for distinction." In particular, young Abe Lincoln aspired to achieve something beyond material success. He hoped his accomplishments would make the world a better place, to the extent that he would be "truly esteemed of my fellow men, by rendering myself worthy of their esteem."[2]

He believed that the career that gave him the best chance to achieve such a lofty goal was in the political arena, and at the age

---

1. Dirck, *Lincoln the Lawyer* (Champaign: University of Illinois Press, 2007), 3.

2. Abraham Lincoln, political announcement at New Salem, Illinois, March 9, 1832, accessed September 14, 2011, http://showcase.netins.net/web/creative/lincoln/speeches/1832.htm.

of twenty-five, after serving his first term in the Illinois General Assembly, Abraham Lincoln decided the best way to develop superior political skills was by practicing law.

Among other things, from his early legislative experience, Lincoln knew intuitively that successful politicians must have the following:

- The capacity to win arguments consistently (and he could see no better training ground for honing that skill than being a lawyer).
- The power to communicate with clarity both verbally and in writing, to a broad cross-section of people (and he surely knew that no job provides the daily opportunity for engaging in effective oral and written communication as does being a trial and appellate lawyer).
- The ability to obtain information from others by asking the right questions in an intelligible way as to be responsively answered by people with different levels of intellectual horsepower (and no one asks more questions of more different types of people than a litigator, who in Lincoln's era went to trial several times a month).
- The diligence to research and investigate an issue to ensure that one's ultimate position on a political issue rests on solid ground (and no commercial activity of his time required thorough research and investigative skills more than being a trial lawyer).
- The emotional intelligence to handle sticky political situations with both firmness and grace (and no one traverses challenging interpersonal terrain more often than the trial lawyer).
- And finally, the scholarship necessary to analyze and enact laws that pass constitutional muster and challenge those that don't (and this essential legislative tool is only found in the toolkit of the accomplished appellate lawyer).

So between the ages of twenty-five and twenty-eight, Abraham Lincoln studied on his own (i.e., no law school, no apprenticeship) to become a lawyer, reading Blackstone's *Commentaries* and any other law book he could get his hands on, until becoming "enrolled" to practice law in Illinois on March 1, 1837, after completing his second term in the Illinois legislature.

Of the forty-four presidents of the United States, twenty-six have been lawyers, and Abraham Lincoln tried more cases than any of them. And because every aspect of his life has received thorough historical coverage, there is an abundance of stories, coming primarily from his final law partner William Herndon and his fellow circuit rider Henry Clay Whitney (who both wrote books about Lincoln after his death), which serve to flesh out the voluminous archived documentation contained in the Lincoln Legal Papers housed in Springfield, Illinois. Together, the stories and records present a clear picture of how Mr. Lincoln practiced law.

From 1837 until he suspended his practice in 1860 to focus on the presidential election, Lincoln and his partners handled over five thousand matters, tried over one thousand jury cases to verdict, and argued over four hundred cases to the Illinois Supreme Court, meaning Honest Abe worked his lanky frame to the bone during his twenty-one years as an active lawyer (losing two years of practice in 1847–1848 during his one term in Congress).

He had extraordinary versatility, the scope of his practice ranging from representing criminal defendants in murder trials to being counsel for major railroad companies in their most important cases, while performing in the full ambit of tribunals—from lowly Illinois justices of the peace all the way to the U.S. Supreme Court. To have the volume of work necessary to bring in a steady stream of fees, more than any other type of case, Lincoln handled mundane debt-collection lawsuits (representing creditors in roughly two-thirds of them), thus accepting the reality that being a lawyer requires grinding through tedious matters with the same diligence and professionalism required of attorneys in complex cases.

Sometime during the second half of his legal career, at an unknown date in the 1850s, Abraham Lincoln composed his "Notes for a Lecture on Law," which provide his six best pieces of advice to lawyers entering the profession. He probably delivered these remarks in a speech to a bar association, though there's no record of it. Those historians who have analyzed his career[3] since the compilation of the Lincoln Legal Papers have concluded that Lincoln's walk matched his talk as a lawyer. Lincoln's six points of advice follow over the course of the next several pages.

———————

The leading rule for the lawyer, as for the man of every other calling, is diligence. Leave nothing for to-morrow which can be done to-day. Never let your correspondence fall behind. Whatever piece of business you have in hand, before stopping, do all the labor pertaining to it which can then be done. When you bring a common-law suit, if you have the facts for doing so, write the declaration at once. If a law point be involved, examine the books, and note the authority you rely on upon the declaration itself, where you are sure to find it when wanted. The same of defenses and pleas. In business not likely to be litigated—ordinary collection cases, foreclosures, partitions, and the like—make all examinations of titles, and note them, and even draft orders and decrees in advance. This course has a triple advantage; it avoids omissions and neglect, saves your labor when once done, performs the labor out of court when you have leisure, rather than in court when you have not.[4]

Abraham Lincoln's diligence as a lawyer is linked to his strong work ethic, reflected by the previously enumerated volume of cases he and his three partners[5] handled from 1837 to 1860. His last partner, William Herndon, said that when necessary, Lincoln worked

———————

3. The three leading books (in chronological order) on Lincoln's legal career published since 2000, when the Lincoln Legal Papers were assembled, are Allen D. Spiegel's *A. Lincoln, Esquire: A Shrewd, Sophisticated Lawyer in His Time* (Macon, GA: Mercer University Press, 2002); Mark E. Steiner's *An Honest Calling: The Law Practice of Abraham Lincoln* (DeKalb: Northern Illinois University Press, 2006); and Brian Dirck's *Lincoln the Lawyer.*

4. Abraham Lincoln's Notes for a Law Lecture, accessed September 27, 2011, http://showcase.netins.net/web/creative/lincoln/speeches/lawlect.htm.

5. From 1837 to 1841, Lincoln partnered with John Todd Stuart (a cousin of Mary Todd, who became Lincoln's wife in 1842); from 1841 to 1844, with Stephen T. Logan; and from 1844 to 1860, with William Herndon.

from 7 A.M. till midnight. To maintain his income throughout the year, he traveled the circuit of counties around Springfield, living on the road six out of every twelve months, while advertising his services in local newspapers and representing clients on opposite sides of legal issues,[6] business issues,[7] and even moral issues,[8] meaning Lincoln took business as it came and didn't turn it away for philosophical reasons.

Though he did not read law for recreation, he was well known for zeroing in on any case, treatise, or digest that provided support for a client's position. His second partner, Stephen Logan, claimed that Lincoln prepared for trials by studying individual cases, rather than through general study of the law. According to Logan, "He got to be a pretty good lawyer though his general knowledge of law was never very formidable. But he would study out his case and make about as much of it as anybody."[9]

William Herndon explained that it was in the Supreme Court of Illinois that Lincoln was truly a great lawyer. After all, appellate work gave Lincoln ample time to read the record, gather the facts of the case, and search for applicable law.

Extemporaneous speaking should be practiced and cultivated. It is the lawyer's avenue to the public. However able and faithful he may be in other respects, people are slow to bring him business if he cannot make a speech. And yet there is not a more fatal error to young lawyers than relying too much on speech-making. If any one, upon his

---

6. In different cases representing different clients at different times before the Illinois Supreme Court, Lincoln argued for and against the proposition that evidence of a defendant's net worth should be admissible to a jury in assessing damages.

7. Lincoln represented railroads and sued railroads.

8. In one case, he represented a slave owner attempting to reclaim his slaves after they became domiciled in the free state of Illinois and in another case represented an abolitionist charged with assisting runaway slaves.

9. Mark Steiner, *An Honest Calling*, 41.

rare powers of speaking, shall claim an exemption from
the drudgery of the law, his case is a failure in advance.[10]

From a young age, Abraham Lincoln enjoyed public speaking.
As a child, he was known to entertain his peers by standing on a tree
stump and reciting verbatim (thanks to his photographic memory)
the contents of sermons he had heard in his parents' church. He
undoubtedly enjoyed oratory early on because he was good at it and
received praise for his performances.

Lincoln began making political speeches in 1832 when he first
ran for the Illinois legislature. Although he was not elected (finishing
eighth in a field of thirteen), in the area where he gave most of his
speeches during the campaign—around New Salem, where he lived
from 1831 to 1837—he received 277 out of the 300 votes cast.

Over the remainder of his life before being elected president,
outside of his extemporaneous speaking as a trial and appellate lawyer, and in addition to stand-alone political speeches, Abe Lincoln enjoyed recreational debating and giving public lectures on topics ranging from reverence for law (in his speech entitled "The Perpetuation
of Our Political Institutions" to the Young Men's Lyceum of Springfield in 1838), to the history of man's progress (in a speech entitled
"Discoveries and Inventions," given in and around Springfield in the
late 1850s), to the clear preference of our Founding Fathers for the
federal government's having sole jurisdiction to determine the extent
of slavery's expansion in new American states and territories (at his
address in New York City at Cooper Union in early 1860, the three-
and-a-half-hour speech that led to his being nominated for president
that year by the Republican Party).

In making his point about the importance of lawyers practicing public speaking, Lincoln recognized (at the paragraph's end) the
temptation that a skilled orator has of becoming so enamored with
his own voice as to believe that his virtuosity with the spoken word al-
lows him to skimp on preparation. To resist that temptation, Lincoln
stressed the need to always keep one's nose to the grindstone.

---

10. Abraham Lincoln's Notes for a Law Lecture, accessed September 27, 2011, http://showcase.
netins.net/web/creative/lincoln/speeches/lawlect.htm.

Discourage litigation. Persuade your neighbors to compromise whenever you can. Point out to them how the
nominal winner is often a real loser—in fees, expenses,
and waste of time. As a peacemaker, the lawyer has a superior opportunity of being a good man. There will still
be business enough.[11]

Abraham Lincoln recognized the trial lawyer's duty to provide
candid advice, making sure he never gave a client false hope for a lawsuit's probable outcome. William Herndon explained that Lincoln's
general way of doing business entailed listening to the client's story
and then thinking awhile before giving his opinion. When he did
give his opinion—which he sometimes did not do until having first
researched applicable law—he would clearly and honestly tell the client, "You are in the right," or "You are in the wrong."[12]

In particular, debtor-creditor cases lent themselves to prompt
settlement. Much local business in the pre–Civil War era was trans-
acted through credit, and when a default occurred, the defendant's typical defense was "hard times," meaning the debtor often
couldn't afford a lawyer, putting the plaintiff in a position to get
an uncollectible judgment. Working out a settlement under this
frequent scenario was the most logical way to proceed. When debt-
ors or anyone else came to Lincoln with notions of asserting a spuri-
ous defense, Lincoln would openly tell them that they had no case,
and he would immediately advocate settlement.

Never stir up litigation. A worse man can scarcely be
found than one who does this. Who can be more nearly
a fiend than he who habitually overhauls the register of
deeds in search of defects in titles, whereon to stir up
strife, and put money in his pocket? A moral tone ought
to be infused into the profession which should drive such
men out of it.[13]

---

11. Ibid.

12. Steiner, *An Honest Calling*, 58.

13. Abraham Lincoln's Notes for a Law Lecture, accessed September 27, 2011, http://showcase.
netins.net/web/creative/lincoln/speeches/lawlect.htm.

There's a difference between a lawyer marketing himself to attract business (as Lincoln did through newspaper advertising and public speaking) and his proactively generating a lawsuit between people with no prior knowledge of there being a dispute. In Lincoln's time, many lawyers with insufficient business to make ends meet attempted to create work by searching courthouse records for title defects in hopes of turning them into a case. Lincoln would have none of that, believing such activities damaged the reputation of the profession. In any era, lawyers are supposed to be in the business of resolving disputes, not creating them.

The matter of fees is important, far beyond the mere question of bread and butter involved. Properly attended to, fuller justice is done to both lawyer and client. An exorbitant fee should never be claimed. As a general rule never take your whole fee in advance, nor any more than a small retainer. When fully paid beforehand, you are more than a common mortal if you can feel the same interest in the case, as if something was still in prospect for you, as well as for your client. And when you lack interest in the case the job will very likely lack skill and diligence in the performance. Settle the amount of fee and take a note in advance. Then you will feel that you are working for something, and you are sure to do your work faithfully and well. Never sell a fee note—at least not before the consideration service is performed. It leads to negligence and dishonesty—negligence by losing interest in the case, and dishonesty in refusing to refund when you have allowed the consideration to fail.[14]

In the final years of his legal career, in the late 1850s, Lincoln averaged an annual income of between $4,000 and $5,000 (sizable enough in those days to live in a nice home and support his family comfortably), gained on flat fees that typically ranged from $2.50

----

14. Ibid.

to $50. The biggest fee he ever made on a case was $5,000, by successfully representing the Illinois Central Railroad on a tax challenge that resulted in saving his client hundreds of thousands of dollars, though Lincoln ended up having to sue the railroad to get the fee. His philosophy on fees in this paragraph about why a lawyer should not collect the bulk of his fees in advance (to stay focused and motivated on the client's matter) surely was a factor in Lincoln's having to sue clients seventeen times to be paid in full.

Getting paid for work while riding the circuit was especially problematical. Lincoln would often get hired as he rode into a town by someone he didn't know and would have to agree to a fee arrangement quickly before court opened for business.

This philosophy of not getting most of his fee up front certainly kept Lincoln constantly hungry for new business and drove him to achieve the best possible results, since losing a case usually caused clients to deem an outstanding legal debt balance not due and payable.

> There is a vague popular belief that lawyers are necessarily dishonest. I say vague, because when we consider to what extent confidence and honors are reposed in and conferred upon lawyers by the people, it appears improbable that their impression of dishonesty is very distinct and vivid. Yet the impression is common, almost universal. Let no young man choosing the law for a calling for a moment yield to the popular belief—resolve to be honest at all events; and if in your own judgment you cannot be an honest lawyer, resolve to be honest without being a lawyer. Choose some other occupation, rather than one in the choosing of which you do, in advance, consent to be a knave.[15]

Lincoln concluded his advice with the most essential point— the importance of a lawyer's maintaining honesty in his dealings.

---

15. Ibid.

What separated Abraham Lincoln from most of the legal pack was his perspective that a lawyer must not only be honest in his business dealings but also must have intellectual honesty in his courtroom presentations—i.e., in making an argument to a judge, jury, or appellate court, an attorney must never misrepresent his opponent's position by playing fast and loose with its contents.

Lincoln believed the intellectually honest approach was the best way to win an argument in court, in politics, or anywhere else. His standard method of defeating an opponent was to begin by accurately reciting the entirety of his adversary's position, demonstrating why it was flawed, and then establishing why his position made more sense. In Lincoln's era, trial lawyers were judged by their forthrightness, force of intellect, power of oratory, ability to put on a good forensic show, and competitiveness at trial. In that string of necessary characteristics, first and foremost was the need to be *forthright*—making points in a straightforward, intellectually honest manner.

Lincoln was known for never engaging in malicious or underhanded practices; nothing about the contents of his arguments was misleading or deceptive. Judge Sidney Breese, who presided over many cases that Lincoln handled, commented:

> I have for a quarter of a century regarded Mr. Lincoln as the finest lawyer I ever knew, and of a professional bearing so high-toned and honorable, as justly, and without derogating from the claims of others, entitling him to be presented to the profession as a model well worthy of the closest imitation.[16]

There is clear and abundant evidence that over the course of more than two decades, Abraham Lincoln conducted himself as a lawyer in accordance with the advice he presented in his "Notes for a Lecture on Law." In 2009, providing commentary for the Library of Congress's exhibition "With Malice toward None," former U.S. Supreme Court justice Sandra Day O'Connor confirmed that Lincoln's

---

16. Francis Fisher Browne, *The Every-day Life of Abraham Lincoln*, (New York: N. D. Thompson Publishing Co., 1887), 234.

"notes for advice to lawyers are as timely and wise today as when he wrote them in the 1850s."[17]

Then, one day in early 1861, Abraham Lincoln went from being a trial and appellate lawyer to being sworn in as the sixteenth president of the United States. The lessons learned from Lincoln's entire life, not just his legal career, greatly enhance the ultimate guidance he provides the profession.[18]

––––––––––

On February 12, 1809, Abraham Lincoln entered the world in poverty, born of a mother who would die before her son reached the age of ten and an unambitious illiterate father from whom the boy would soon become estranged. Despite Lincoln's starting out life in such forboding circumstances, he is now recognized by most historians as the greatest president in American history.

In reading and synthesizing the six leading critically acclaimed biographies of Abraham Lincoln published in the last few years,[19] I have identified four essential characteristics in the man that empowered his unique greatness and cause him to be lifted up today as a timeless hero for lawyers:

Astounding brainpower. Abraham Lincoln had superhuman powers of concentration, comprehension, discernment, and communication.

As a boy, Lincoln read every book he could get his hands on. Though the quantity of books available to young Abraham in rural Kentucky and Indiana where he grew up was limited, the quality was high—most notably, the King James Bible, Aesop's fables, Shakespeare's plays, Ben Franklin's autobiography, and Bunyan's *The*

17. Harold Holzer and Joshua Wolf Shenk, eds., *In Lincoln's Hand: His Original Manuscripts* (New York: Bantam Dell, 2009), 45.

18. An earlier version of the following text by Talmage Boston was published in *Texas Bar Journal* in February 2009.

19. The biographies upon which I relied for drawing my conclusions are James McPherson, *Tried by War: Abraham Lincoln as Commander-in-Chief* (New York: Penguin Press, 2008); Doris Kearns Goodwin, *Team of Rivals: The Political Genius of Abraham Lincoln* (New York: Simon & Schuster, 2005); Fred Kaplan, *Lincoln: The Biography of a Writer* (New York: HarperCollins, 2008); William Lee Miller, *Lincoln's Virtues: An Ethical Biography* (New York: Alfred A. Knopf, 2002); William Lee Miller, *President Lincoln: The Duty of a Statesman* (New York: Alfred A. Knopf, 2008); and Joshua Wolf Shenk, *Lincoln's Melancholy: How Depression Challenged a President and Fueled His Greatness* (New York: Houghton Mifflin, 2005).

Pilgrim's Progress. Young Lincoln not only read these timeless master-pieces, he reread them many times and then memorized large chunks of them, providing the foundation for his ultimate literary eloquence.

This desire to learn and master complicated material was not just a childhood phenomenon but in fact lasted throughout Lincoln's lifetime. Over the course of his adult years, on his own, always with his head in a book, he mastered topics ranging from law, to Euclidean geometry, to military strategy, to foreign policy, to the verses of leading European poets.

Consistent with his lifelong reading obsession, as a lawyer and a politician, Lincoln earned a reputation for thoroughly researching and considering all sides of an issue before forming his final opinion. And that opinion would gel only after Lincoln had spent extended time in solitude, never delegating his critical thinking to others. The president's secretary, John Nicolay, described Lincoln's writing methods as a process of "cumulative thought," which entailed reducing complex ideas to paragraphs and sentences, then polishing or elaborating those passages on subsequent reading.

Once reaching a conclusion on a subject, because of his deep thinking process associated with getting there, Lincoln held fast to his convictions and never flip-flopped. In one of his biographies, University of Virginia history professor William Lee Miller confirms the steadfastness of Lincoln's opinions once he had formed them, as reflected by an incident in which the president confronted Frederick Douglass on his allegation that Lincoln's position on slavery had been slow and vacillating. Although Lincoln made no objection to the word *slow*, he did object to *vacillating*, telling Douglass, "I think it cannot be shown that when I have once taken a position, I have ever retreated from it."[20]

International relations scholar Hans Morgenthau cements the first characteristic behind Lincoln's greatness, which elevated him above his peers: "His sheer brainpower must have exceeded that of all other presidents, Jefferson included. . . . That extraordinary intelligence revealed itself in philosophic understanding of public issues, in a judicious concern with

---

20. Miller, *Lincoln's Virtues*, 14.

politically relevant detail, in a mastery of political manipulation, in military judgment."[21]

Absolute self-control. Abraham Lincoln maintained squeaky clean living habits and the highest integrity throughout his life.

Though he grew up in a world where most of his male contemporaries used tobacco, imbibed alcohol, conversed with profanity, and gambled, Abraham Lincoln never engaged in such vices. According to Lincoln biographer Fred Kaplan, Lincoln refused to partake because vices reflect "those aspects of human nature that prevent the triumph of reason and moral vision."[22]

Not only did these vices stand in the way of Lincoln's altruistic mental activities, but the most favored (and time-consuming) physical recreational activities of his era—hunting and fishing—also stood in the way of his making the progress he expected in his career, such that in furtherance of his ambitious goals, Lincoln rejected hunting and fishing as well. Outside of time spent socializing with friends, to the extent free time existed in any day, Lincoln used it one and only one way: for reading.

In accordance with his abstinence from vices, Lincoln maintained steady integrity throughout his lifetime, receiving his famous nickname "Honest Abe" the old-fashioned way: he earned it. As a twenty-three-year-old man in Indiana, Lincoln became part owner of a small-town country store that went out of business, leaving him with many creditors and no apparent way to repay them. Over the ten years following the closing, as he pursued a new career as a lawyer, Lincoln scrimped and made the necessary personal sacrifices that allowed him finally to repay one hundred cents on the dollar to those he owed, even though his creditors had not pressed him to make them whole.

In his new career as a lawyer and later as a politician, his integrity continued to prevail, as Lincoln insisted on presenting arguments steeped in unequivocal intellectual honesty, never playing fast and

---

21. Hans J. Morgenthau and David Hein, *Essays on Lincoln's Faith and Politics*, vol. 4 (Lanham, MD: University Press of America, 1983), 59.

22. Kaplan, *Lincoln: The Biography of a Writer*, 114.

loose with facts, knowing that shading the truth would surely prove counterproductive to establishing his position.

For a final example of Lincoln's steadfast integrity, as a husband with a verbally (and on occasion physically) abusive and mentally unstable wife, Lincoln maintained fidelity every day of his marriage.

Emotional intelligence. Abraham Lincoln had a uniquely high capacity to deal with his peers effectively.

As impressive as his commitment to resisting vices and little white lies, Lincoln's lifelong surge toward full-blown greatness was also fueled by what modern psychologists call "emotional intelligence," defined most notably by author Daniel Goleman as the capacity to maintain self-awareness, control one's emotions and impulses amidst changing circumstances, empathize with and react to others' emotions, and manage relationships even when in conflict.

For a common man to maintain emotional intelligence on a daily basis requires absolute self-control and consummate tact. To maintain it in the midst of serving as commander-in-chief during the Civil War while attending to an increasingly deranged wife and grieving over the death of a treasured ten-year-old son required almost a divine level of self-awareness, emotional control, and capacity to harmonize disparate factions.

As revealed by his most esteemed contemporary biographers, the hallmarks of Lincoln's ability to stay in a mode of steady emotional-intelligence equilibrium while leading the country at its time of greatest turbulence are best evidenced by the following:

- Regardless of others' blunders that set back the Union cause during the war, Lincoln did not engage in blaming, denigrating, or fault finding. Occasionally, he would write letters that fully vented his feelings toward those generals who had let him down, but he would not mail them.
- At the outset of his presidency, those with more education and political experience than Lincoln would often level insults at him, perceiving that someone so unsophisticated

and inexperienced could not possibly be up to the job. Never did Lincoln take the bait and retaliate, or even hold a grudge, recognizing at all times that "I shall do nothing in malice. What I deal with is too vast for malicious dealing."[23]

- In the daily hurly-burly of war and politics that provoked constant criticism and genuine fear of losing the American dream of republic, Lincoln remained stoic and never panicked. Knowing the power of words, the president insisted that his public and private messages at all times were concise, clear, apt, logical, and carefully edited. Misunderstandings arising from ambiguous communications simply had to be avoided at such a critical time.

- Despite holding the powerful office of president, Lincoln's ego stayed in check. Exhibiting arrogance, acting in a mode of self-righteousness, and putting down lesser men were attitudes that apparently never entered his mind.

A high sense of purpose. Abraham Lincoln would not be satisfied with his life unless and until he had made a positive difference in the world.

Unlike his father, Abraham Lincoln had no desire to work with his hands in farming or carpentry but instead aspired to rise and gain distinction by making a living with and fully utilizing his mind. The word *autodidact*, used frequently by biographer Kaplan, is defined as a person who is "self-taught and self-educated." A knowledgeable lexicographer would put a photograph of Lincoln next to that word and its definition, as it is difficult to imagine anyone teaching himself more than our sixteenth president did.

Imagine homeschooling oneself on "the law" with no instructor or mentor and reaching a level of proficiency not just to the extent of being admitted to the bar but also to try major lawsuits and argue appeals all the way to the U.S. Supreme Court. Imagine mastering military history and battle tactics relying on books borrowed from the Library of Congress so as to be several steps ahead of generals

---

23. Abraham Lincoln, Letter to Cuthbert Bullitt, July 28, 1862, accessed September 26, 2011, http://showcase.netins.net/web/creative/lincoln/speeches/persevere.htm.

who had graduated from West Point. Imagine having such total command of the Bible and Shakespeare as to be able to quote exactly the right passages at the most opportune time whether in court or on the political stage without having attended a seminary or a university. Abraham Lincoln pushed himself and rose to the highest human plane so as to do all those things—on his own, without ever being mentored by a parent, teacher, colleague, or superior.

And all this high-powered self-education provided the foundation for Lincoln's constant ascent toward larger opportunities. According to William Lee Miller, Lincoln became confident that he could locate in books whatever information he required, and "that confidence in his powers of understanding what was written on the page seems to have encouraged a broader self-confidence, in his judgment and his critical powers—let us call it a moral self-confidence."[24]

Having established the bona fides of Lincoln's advancement from his humble beginnings—and the ferocious zeal of his self-education, which gave him the confidence to take his skill set to the next level at every step of life's road—Lincoln knew that to do something of such significance as to be remembered by his fellow man, he had to hitch his wagon load of talent to a star political issue that captivated the national populace. He did just that when he seized upon the issue of stopping the spread of slavery by becoming the leading opponent of the Kansas-Nebraska Act in 1854.

When Lincoln learned that Congress had passed the Kansas-Nebraska Act, he became "thunderstruck" by its proslavery and nationally divisive effect, and he refused to rest until he had done everything in his power to have it nullified. His personal crusade on the issue of stopping slavery's expansion lasted through his becoming elected president in November 1860. In the course of those six years, he gained a national following from his participation in the Lincoln-Douglas debates (which had the issue as their focus), allowing him to emerge and speak throughout the northern part of the

---

24. Miller, *Lincoln's Virtues*, 53.

country as the most persuasive and eloquent spokesman on the era's most controversial issue.

Upon Lincoln's getting elected president, Southern states immediately began to secede from the Union, followed by South Carolina's army attacking Fort Sumter, necessitating Lincoln's high sense of "purpose" on the issue of stopping slavery's expansion to shift toward an even higher priority, one that flowed from his responsibilities assumed upon taking the presidential oath of office. Effective March 4, 1861, President Abraham Lincoln's new highest "purpose" in life was to restore the United States of America to an indivisible country governed as a republic by majority rule.

Lincoln's ferocious and purposeful resolve to restore the Union, beginning on the day he took on the office of president, became such a personal crusade that if bringing about this desired result required suspending the right to habeas corpus for a short time to prevent border state Maryland from seceding, then the president of the United States would do what it took, rationalizing the temporary infringement of constitutional rights on the basis that "often a limb must be amputated to save a life."[25]

As the war went on into 1862, with no end in sight, Lincoln combined what had become his two driving "purposes" (restoring the Union and ending slavery) by writing and then signing into law the Emancipation Proclamation on January 1, 1863, using the enactment of a law that provided the impetus to release slaves from their Southern owners (who at the time did not recognize federal law, since they no longer resided in the United States but rather lived in the Confederate States of America) as a means of motivating African American men to consider the possibility of leaving their owners and joining the Union army, thereby adding additional strength to his troops to overpower the Confederate army, end the war, restore the Union, and prohibit slavery altogether. As he prepared to sign the Emancipation Proclamation, the president acknowledged to those present that he knew in his heart, after a lifetime of striving, that he had finally done something that would

    25. Abraham Lincoln, Letter to Albert G. Hodges, April 4, 1864, accessed September 26, 2011, http://showcase.netins.net/web/creative/lincoln/speeches/hodges.htm.

be recognized as a landmark moment in history, thereby fulfilling the "purpose" and achieving his goal of being "truly esteemed
of my fellow men, by rendering myself worthy of their esteem." His
exact words at the time were, "I never, in my life, felt more certain
that I was doing right, than I do in signing this paper. If my name
ever goes into history it will be for this act, and my whole soul is in
it."[26]

———————

In the course of researching and writing her book *Team of Rivals*, Doris Kearns Goodwin spent a decade focused on the subject
of Abraham Lincoln. Through reading Lincoln's own writings and
what others wrote about him and from studying and assessing his life
story, Goodwin ultimately found "that after nearly two centuries, the
uniquely American story of Abraham Lincoln has unequalled power
to captivate the imagination and to inspire emotion."[27] It is for this
reason that the life of Abraham Lincoln should continue to matter
to us today.

ATTICUS FINCH

There's no record that Harper Lee was knowledgeable about the
particulars of Abraham Lincoln's life at the time she created Atticus
Finch. As is demonstrated later in this chapter, Ms. Lee developed
and acknowledged the character as a thinly fictionalized version of
her father, Amasa Lee. The parallels between Messrs. Lincoln and
Finch, however, go well beyond their choosing the same profession
and being able to practice law while serving in the legislature. Among
other things, they match up in the following areas:

Education. Lincoln famously had less than one year of formal
education. It is mentioned in *Mockingbird* that Atticus never went to
school.

Preparation for legal career. Since neither went to law school and

———————

26. Goodwin, *A Team of Rivals*, 499.

27. Ibid., xix.

neither apprenticed with a senior lawyer, both learned the trade by the act of "reading law."

Lifestyle and hobbies. What Scout says about Atticus at the beginning of chapter 10 could have been said by Lincoln's children: "He did not do the things our schoolmates' fathers did: he never went hunting, he did not play poker or fish or drink or smoke. He sat in the livingroom and read."[28]

Income. Both of them derived a reasonable income from the law and had no outside entrepreneurial activities.

Self-control. When provoked, neither Lincoln nor Finch raised his voice in anger or retaliated toward his antagonist.

Parenting style. Mr. Lincoln and Mr. Finch both gave their children essentially total freedom to explore life and imposed little discipline on them.

Conscience. As president, Lincoln claimed that he wished to conduct his administration in such a way "that if, at the end when I come to lay down the reins of power, I have lost every other friend on earth, I shall at least have one friend left, and that friend shall be down inside of me."[29]

In *Mockingbird*, Atticus provides this justification to Scout on why he's representing Tom Robinson, "Before I can live with other folks, I've got to live with myself. The one thing that doesn't abide by majority rule is a person's conscience."[30]

Great lawyering using unexpected evidence. Abe Lincoln established Duff Armstrong's innocence using the *Farmer's Almanac* to prove that the moon was *not* high on the night the victim was murdered, thereby disproving the testimony of the crime's eyewitness. Similarly, Atticus Finch established Tom Robinson's innocence by showing that the defendant's crippled left arm could not possibly

---

28. Harper Lee, *To Kill a Mockingbird* (Philadelphia: J. P. Lippincott, 1960; New York: Warner Books, 1982), 94. Citations are to the Warner edition.

29. Ida M. Tarbell, *The Life of Abraham Lincoln*, vol. 3 (New York: Lincoln History Society, 1895), 175.

30. Lee, *Mockingbird*, 109.

have been used to beat the right side of Mayella Ewell's face, thereby disproving the testimony of the victim's father, Bob Ewell.

Attitude toward African Americans. Frederick Douglass claimed that he was completely at ease in Lincoln's presence, for Lincoln "did not let me feel for a moment that there was any difference in the color of our skins."[31] When Scout asked Atticus if he was a "nigger-lover," Atticus responded that he certainly was, for he did his best to love everybody.

Appreciation by the African American community. Shortly before Lee's surrender at Appomattox, the president traveled to Richmond unannounced. As he walked the streets, African Americans in the city spontaneously commenced having a parade in Lincoln's honor, some calling out to him as "Father Abraham" and others bowing at his knee. This reaction to the Great Emancipator compares favorably to the reception by Maycomb's black community given to Atticus when he gave his all on behalf of Tom Robinson. Reverend Sykes tells Scout that his church has no better friend than Atticus Finch. Later, the pastor leads all African Americans sitting on the courtroom balcony to stand in honor of Atticus as he passes below them, following the trial's conclusion.

Recognition of racial injustice's consequences. By the end of the Civil War, which caused over 600,000 soldiers to lose their lives, Lincoln determined that such a holocaust was the proximate result of Americans' having allowed the institution of slavery to be permitted within our boundaries for so long. His Second Inaugural Address delivered one month before the war's end explains his perception of this cause-and-effect situation. After Tom Robinson's conviction by an all-white jury, despite clear evidence of his innocence, Atticus Finch provides his cause-and-effect analysis to his son, Jem. He assures his son that "it's all adding up and one of these days we're going to pay the bill for it."[32]

---

31. Goodwin, *Team of Rivals*, 650.

32. Lee, *Mockingbird*, 223.

With all these similarities in human experiences and attitudes, it's not surprising that Abraham Lincoln and Atticus Finch practiced law from a common perspective of high professionalism.[33]

On July 11, 1960, first-time author Harper Lee threw a small, flat, 296-page stone into the ocean of literature and set off a tidal wave that reverberates to this day. Philadelphia-based publisher J. P. Lippincott released *To Kill a Mockingbird* to instant critical acclaim and a place atop the fiction bestseller list, where it would stay for eighty weeks.

Among other things, Lee's book won the Pulitzer Prize in 1961; became the subject of a successful movie that opened in December 1962, with Atticus Finch played by Gregory Peck in the only Academy Award–winning role of his career; and sold over 30 million copies in over forty languages, making it history's seventh all-time bestselling novel.

In addition to its commercial success, through Lee's writing and Peck's acting, the character Atticus Finch has now pointed many generations toward the goal of becoming lawyers—and not just run-of-the-mill lawyers but lawyers aspiring to serve the bar with an Atticus Finch level of integrity, professionalism, and courage.

Question: Was Atticus Finch purely a creature of Harper Lee's imagination, or was he a real person in her life thinly disguised under a fictional name?

Answer: The latter.

AMASA LEE AS ATTICUS FINCH, HARPER LEE AS SCOUT

Shortly after *Mockingbird*'s publication, Harper Lee acknowledged that Atticus Finch was essentially a favorably fictionalized version of her father, Amasa Coleman Lee (who, like Atticus, had an unusual three-syllable name starting with *A*), husband to Francis

---

Facing page: Harper Lee and her father Amasa Lee. Photographer: Donald Uhrbrock. Photo courtesy of Getty Images.

33. An earlier version of the following text by Talmage Boston was published in *Texas Bar Journal* in June 2010.

Cunningham Finch (meaning Atticus's last name was the author's mother's maiden name). In one of her interviews shortly after the publication of *Mockingbird*, before she ceased talking to the media in 1965, Ms. Lee said she portrayed Atticus exactly as she thought of her father Amasa: a man "who has genuine humility and it lends him a natural dignity. He has absolutely no ego drive, and so he is one of the most beloved men in this part of the state."[34]

Named by Ms. Lee after Cicero's friend, Titus Pomponius Atticus, father Atticus and father Amasa matched up identically in the following respects:

- Both were small-town lawyers in Alabama who served in the state legislature.
- Both had children who called them by their first name, instead of "Dad" or "Papa."
- Both were sole parent mentors to their children, as Atticus's wife died when his children were young, and Amasa's wife fell into a mental illness funk that rendered her homebound and speechless when her children were young, totally disconnecting her from the family until her death in 1951.
- Both served as counsel for African American defendants accused of committing felonies against white people in highly publicized small-town trials in Alabama. Despite their best efforts, their clients were found guilty by all-white juries, resulting in what proved to be death sentences.
- Both had the courage as white men to stare down racist threats and thereby stand up for the rights of black people in a segregated society long before the days of Jackie Robinson, Rosa Parks, and *Brown v. Board of Education*.

If Amasa Lee became Atticus Finch, then Nelle Harper Lee[35] (born in 1926) portrayed herself as *Mockingbird*'s protagonist, Jean Louise ("Scout") Finch—a preadolescent tomboy in the 1930s

---

34. Kerry Madden, *Up Close: Harper Lee: A Twentieth-Century Life* (New York: Viking, 2009), 152.

35. Throughout her life in all social situations, the author has been called by her first name and used her middle name only when she wrote for publication.

raised by a father without any maternal affection, who learned to read sitting on her dad's lap, while inhabiting a small Alabama town where wild dogs sometimes roamed the streets and a belligerent old woman sat on her front porch and screamed at children passing by. Like Scout, the author enjoyed the company of a peculiar summer-time male friend (her childhood buddy, Truman Capote, became *Mockingbird*'s Dill Harris) and was intrigued by a young man on her street mysteriously imprisoned in his own home (Lee's neighbor, Son Boleware, became *Mockingbird*'s Boo Radley).

Thus, the "fictional" characters who lived in "make-believe" Maycomb, Alabama, during the Great Depression became real to *Mockingbird*'s readers because the book, in fact, was an account of real people who lived in the real town of Monroeville, Alabama, during the Great Depression. Whereas best-selling author Pat Conroy had the characters who inhabited his hometown of Charleston, South Carolina, in his newest novel, *South of Broad* (New York: Doubleday, 2009), say that "somewhere between 19–27% of what a storyteller says is true, and then you start adding things," *Mockingbird* more than doubled those percentages. The details of Harper and Amasa Lee's lives show that the majority of *Mockingbird* is essentially true, at least through the author's eyes, writing a book twenty years after her childhood that described what she had seen, felt, and remembered about the people and events in her small, racially segregated, and economically depressed Alabama hometown.

ATTICUS'S DEMONSTRATION OF WHAT TO DO IN AND OUT OF THE COURTROOM

The statements and accounts of what Atticus Finch said and did throughout *Mockingbird* established his Lincolnesque persona in the midst of a volatile, racially torn, small-town society, capable of giving only lip service to the concept of equal justice for all. Accused of raping a white adolescent in 1935, Finch's African American client Tom Robinson (thankfully) was not lynched by an angry mob, as he might have been had the alleged crime taken place in the nineteenth century. No, Mr. Robinson received a jury trial in a courtroom aided by his court-appointed lawyer,

Mr. Finch—who, surprisingly (in that era), gave the case his best effort. Despite his attorney's stellar defense and evidence that established the defendant's innocence, the trial's outcome was determined before it began. Because Mr. Robinson was black, his alleged victim was white, and everyone on the jury was white, a guilty verdict was inevitably reached.

While living and single-parenting in a segregated community and representing Tom Robinson in a stacked-deck trial, parent and lawyer Atticus Finch has made a lasting impression as a role model on generations of readers and moviegoers. Embracing daily living with the highest integrity, and making the legal profession appear as a career calling of the highest order, Atticus caused many to join the profession, inspired by the following words and deeds:

Duty to the poor. Early in the book, Scout observed her dad give valuable counsel to Walter Cunningham, a man caught in an "entailment," at a time when he was barely able to scratch an existence off the land for the support of his family. When Mr. Cunningham ashamedly tells Atticus that he doesn't know when he'll be able to pay his legal fees, Atticus immediately tries to put his client's mind at ease by telling him that the fee should be the least of his worries.

The value of compromise. When Scout's first-grade teacher ordered her to stop reading at home because her father had "taught [her] all wrong," the angry young girl went home after the reprimand and announced her intention to stop going to school. Lawyer Atticus immediately came up with an alternative dispute-resolution solution by offering her a compromise. Scout agreed to continue attending classes as long as she could continue reading with her father as usual.

Empathy. After Scout complained about her teacher's draconian perspective on reading, lawyer-father Atticus consoled her by offering wisdom on a better way to deal with people. He advised Scout to always try considering things from the other person's perspective, as that would help her relate to all kinds of people.

Later in the book, the lawyer showed a superhuman level of empathy for Bob Ewell, father of Tom Robinson's alleged rape victim, who spat in Atticus's face after being humiliated throughout the trial by testimony that suggested it was Mr. Ewell (not Tom Robinson) who had attacked his daughter. Atticus explained to Scout how he managed not to retaliate after getting hit by Ewell's expectoration. Following his own advice, he had put himself in Bob Ewell's shoes. Atticus had destroyed the man's credibility during the trial, and a man like Bob Ewell needed to lash out in some way. Atticus felt that it was better that he had taken the brunt of the man's anger, rather than Bob Ewell's children.

The need for color-blind justice. When Scout questioned her dad about why he agreed to represent Tom Robinson, Atticus replied that he couldn't have rejected the case and still been able to hold up his head in town. He couldn't even have claimed the moral authority to correct his children if he had refused to assist a black defendant in seeking justice.

Advocate for the legal system. In his closing argument at the trial of Tom Robinson, Mr. Finch gave his version of a Gettysburg Address for the benefit of all *Mockingbird* readers and moviegoers about what our judicial system is supposed to be for everyone who goes to trial or has an appeal in the United States of America. In that speech, he argued that "a court is only as sound as its jury, and a jury is only as sound as the men who make it up."[36] He then implored the men in the jury box to do their duty with impartiality.

Knowing what system failure means. After the jury returned a guilty verdict despite clear evidence of Tom Robinson's innocence, Scout and her brother, Jem, can't begin to process the trial's outcome. Their confusion provided Atticus with the opportunity to give his children a big-picture perspective on racism and how it infects a society when the judicial system fails to achieve justice because of racial prejudice. He tells his children that "the one place where a man ought to get a square deal is in a courtroom, be he any color of the rainbow, but people have a way of carrying their resent-

---

36. Lee, *Mockingbird*, 208.

ments right into a jury box."[37] The system failed Tom Robinson, and Atticus warned his children that they would undoubtedly witness further acts of racism during their lives—one day, however, society would have to pay the price for allowing such things to occur.

AMASA'S EXPERIENCES AS INSPIRATION FOR ATTICUS

Could Amasa Lee have done what Atticus Finch did? Absolutely. We know from the superb (though unauthorized) biography *Mockingbird: A Portrait of Harper Lee* (New York: Henry Holt & Company, 2006) that Mr. Lee performed the following Atticus-like feats in Monroeville, Alabama, when the need arose for a lawyer to stand tall by himself on high moral ground:

- In 1919, after he had practiced law for only four years, and seven years before Harper Lee's birth, Amasa was appointed by the district judge in Monroeville to serve as the lawyer for two black men accused of murdering a white storekeeper. Mr. Lee gave the case his best effort, but the all-white jury returned a guilty verdict, and both defendants were soon hanged. Scout (i.e., Harper Lee) mentioned Atticus having lived through such a situation early in *Mockingbird*.

- Over a nine-month period from November 1933 to July 1934, in a set of facts essentially identical to those of Tom Robinson, a black man named Walter Lett was arrested and later put to trial in the Monroeville County courthouse and convicted by an all-white jury for allegedly raping a white woman, despite strong evidence of the accused's innocence. Amasa Lee wasn't appointed to represent Mr. Lett, but as the editor and publisher of the town's newspaper, the *Monroe Journal*, he followed the case closely from the night of the reported rape through the trial's end. The case was the talk of the town when Harper Lee was eight years old. Amasa surely spoke often to his children about the Lett trial

---

37. Ibid., 223.

from his perspective that our good American judicial system clearly had a notable flaw—it was no better than the judges and juries who served it, many of whom had perspectives clouded by racial prejudice. Though the jury found Walter Lett guilty, and the judge sentenced him to death in the electric chair, the Alabama Board of Pardons reduced the sentence to life imprisonment while the case was pending on appeal, acting at the behest of a letter-writing campaign from citizens of Monroe County (likely led by Amasa Lee), who felt the evidence had not established the defendant's guilt.

Walter Lett's reduced punishment is reminiscent of the moral victory in Tom Robinson's trial, when Atticus's closing argument caused the jury's deliberations to last much longer than expected. The Finches' neighbor down the street, Maudie Atkinson, explained to Scout why the Tom Robinson trial, despite the guilty verdict, gave hope to those in the enlightened segment of the Maycomb community. Even though the jury didn't arrive at the proper verdict, the fact that the jury had to deliberate for so long on that kind of a case was a "baby step" in the right direction. The reduction of Walter Lett's sentence from the electric chair to life imprisonment was a similar "baby step" for racial justice in Alabama.

• In August 1934, shortly after Walter Lett's death penalty sentence had been reduced to life imprisonment, in the presence of his daughter, Amasa came down off his front porch and confronted the Grand Dragon of the local Ku Klux Klan and ultimately persuaded him to stop his one hundred followers' militant posturing as they walked down the street. Amasa's act of courage surely inspired the scene in *Mockingbird* where Atticus faced down the racist mob that arrived at the Maycomb jailhouse the night before the start of Tom Robinson's trial and sought unsuccessfully to impose their own punishment (and probable lynching) on the defendant. In both instances, one lawyer's courage defused an angry, bigoted, potentially murderous crowd.

THE AFTERMATH AND IMPACT OF *MOCKINGBIRD*

A main cause attributed to Harper Lee's total withdrawal from public life in the mid-1960s was her inability to produce a second novel. She wearied (understandably) of hearing the question asked of her again and again: "When will you write another book?" Though she definitely aspired to write another one, and worked hard to produce it, a second book never came to fruition. Why? Writing novels obviously requires an author who can fully activate his or her imagination to construct made-up worlds inhabited by fictional characters. Some writers have the creative imagination to do it, and some don't. Contrast the requirements for producing multiple novels with what it takes to recount one's childhood in a single memoir—i.e., a sensitivity to one's surroundings, a good memory, and deep reflection. Unfortunately, Harper Lee lacked the imagination to create pure make-believe novels, as opposed to having what it took to write one novelized memoir. She finally admitted that to herself in the year 2000, when at the age of seventy-four, the one-time author privately answered the public's unrelenting question by saying that with *Mockingbird*'s execution and publication, "I said what I had to say."[38]

For the epigraph that precedes her book, Harper Lee chose a quote from British writer Charles Lamb, whose early-nineteenth-century readership was made up largely of preadolescents. In looking back from his adult status into his childhood past, Mr. Lamb said something that resonated with Ms. Lee: "Lawyers, I suppose, were children once." This observation is made more intelligible at www.HarperLee.com in the context that "children are born with an instinct for justice and absorb prejudices in the socialization process."[39] What set Atticus Finch and Amasa Lee apart from the rest of the community where they lived was that as lawyers, despite their "socialization process" in Alabama, they would not abandon

---

38. Charles J. Shields, *Mockingbird: A Portrait of Harper Lee* (New York: Henry Holt & Company, 2006), 283.

39. Harper Lee Biography, accessed September 30, 2011, http://www.harperlee.com/bio.htm.

their childlike "instinct for justice," and they refused to allow racial prejudice to enter their psyche at any age.

In the ultimate irony regarding Charles Lamb's quote, *To Kill a Mockingbird* has caused generations of children to look forward and dream of becoming lawyers—and not just average lawyers but lawyers of unimpeachable integrity with an unrelenting focus on achieving true justice. That is, ever since childhood, those touched by *Mockingbird* have wanted to be like Atticus Finch when youth finally passed and the time came to grow up.

————

In summary, the many similarities between Abraham Lincoln and Atticus Finch (aka Amasa Lee) in and out of the courtroom facilitate our appreciating them in tandem, despite their having practiced law in different eras. Their timeless examples provide the prototype for what each member of the profession must embody now to bring lawyers back to the point where society respects our role as thoughtful, honest, and dynamic agents in vigilant pursuit of justice, dispute resolution, and optimum social progress.

CHAPTER TWO

The Two Most Important Lawyers of the Last Fifty Years: Leon Jaworski and James A. Baker, III

Reasonable minds can differ in selecting the two most important lawyers of the last half century. Author's prerogative prevails when a book goes to print.

No higher governing principle exists in the United States than the Rule of Law, which stands for the proposition, "No one is above the law." After developing his skills as a consummate trial and appellate lawyer for almost fifty years, Leon Jaworski prevailed in getting the Rule of Law enforced when he led the Supreme Court to hold in *United States v. Nixon* that "executive privilege" cannot be used by a president to protect himself from prosecution after he commits a crime. Through sagacity and tenacity, the man named "Leonidas" in honor of a courageous Spartan king, and affectionately known as the "Colonel" (his rank in World

---

Facing page: Leon Jaworski. Photographer: Bill Malone. Photo courtesy of Gov. Bill & Vara Daniel Center for Legal History, State Bar of Texas.

War II) at his Houston law firm, brought Richard Nixon to justice in 1974, resulting in the nation's chief executive's having to
resign from office—a unique circumstance in American history.
At that critical time, when the Constitution's separation of powers in our tripartite form of government faced its greatest challenge, Leon Jaworski stepped up to the task of proving that the
Supreme Law of the Land, in fact, *has* checks and balances, and in
the end, the Constitution, as interpreted by the Supreme Court, *has*
final power over everyone—including the president of the United
States.

From 1979 to 1989, James A. Baker, III, went from being an
esteemed business transactional attorney in private practice at
the Andrews Kurth law firm in Houston, Texas, to President
Ronald Reagan's chief of staff, to Reagan's secretary of the treasury,
to President George H. W. Bush's secretary of state, and finally to
Bush's chief of staff. Baker proved to be a quick study in mastering Washington DC's "power game" to the extent that he actually
found a way to get things done in our nation's capital, using the same
interpersonal strengths he had developed as a lawyer negotiating
deals in Houston. Though he excelled in all his government positions, his forty-three months from January 1989 to August 1992
as head of the State Department allowed him to play the role of
world game changer, fully utilizing his legal skills in the international arena as counselor, negotiator, consensus builder, mediator,
and advocate. During that time, (1) Baker pulled America's diplomatic levers into optimum operating position as the Iron Curtain
disintegrated, the Cold War ended, Germany became unified, and
communism fell by the wayside; (2) Iraq's invasion of Kuwait in
the Gulf War was repelled by an international coalition of military forces assembled in large part by Baker; and (3) Israel's leaders met face-to-face and had dialogue with all Arab heads of
state in the Middle East in one venue (Madrid) for the first time
in forty-six years at a meeting Baker organized and orchestrated.
The Madrid Conference soon led to a peace treaty between Jordan
and Israel and began the process that caused the Palestinian
Liberation Organization and Israel to agree to a Declaration of
Principles at the Oslo Accords, thereby moving the tempestuous

Middle East onto a path that may one day lead to some measure of stability.

In short, during the last fifty years, no lawyer played a greater role in preserving the Rule of Law than Leon Jaworski, and no lawyer played a greater role in changing the world for the better than James A. Baker, III. This chapter attempts to recount how these two legal titans (coincidentally both from Texas) succeeded in "raising the bar" to new professional heights in the modern era.

LEON JAWORSKI

> When I pause to contemplate the evil of tampering with the administration of justice—of obstructing it and prostituting it—I think of Saint Thomas More who breathed life into one of the greatest of all obligations of man— that of unswerving loyalty to the ends of justice. Not justice for the affluent and the powerful alone—not justice for the admired and the favored alone—not justice alone for those whose views and beliefs are shared—but justice as well for the weak, for the poor, and even for the despised and the scorned.[1]

Although Leon Jaworski spent the substantial majority of his career as a powerhouse civil litigator at the prominent firm that still bears his name, to him, the most important highlights in his fifty-seven years as a lawyer came as a criminal prosecutor and defender. Yes, he definitely earned a comfortable living and gained high-profile status in Houston, as he won cases before and after World War II for the "King of the Wildcatters," Glenn McCarthy; received a $1 million contingent fee for settling the Moody estate in the late 1950s; and represented Lyndon B. Johnson in 1948 to preserve his election to the United States Senate, and then again in 1960, gaining for his client the right to run simultaneously for the Senate and the vice presidency of the United States (on the ticket with John F.

---

1. Leon Jaworski, "The Most Lustrous Branch: Watergate and the Judiciary," 45 *Fordham L. Rev.* 1267 (1977), http://ir.lawnet.fordham.edu/flr/vol45/iss7/1.

Kennedy). Those achievements in civil cases, however, were small potatoes to Jaworski in the historic scheme of things during his time in the courtroom trenches from 1925 to 1982.

When Leon Jaworski attended Baylor University Law School in 1921, the Ku Klux Klan controlled Waco, Texas. Although a local ordinance had passed that prohibited masked men from parading, when the sheriff tried to enforce it, Klan members smashed his head with their wooden cross. Afterward, the grand jury refused to indict the attackers. In the three years following the incident, social pressure caused more and more people in the Waco area to abandon their principles and join the "Knights of the Invisible Empire." Then, a local white man suspected of being a pimp got seized, tarred, and feathered by a Klan mob, and again the grand jury would not indict anyone for the acts of violence.

Looking back on these events sixty years later, in his memoir *Crossroads*, Leon Jaworski observed, "It was a living lesson to me of what happens to our rights and liberties when forces outside the law take over and begin a merciless rule of terror."[2]

In the midst of Klan lawlessness, Jaworski saw one man in his community with the courage to stand up for the Rule of Law—James P. Alexander, a district judge in Waco, who was one of Jaworski's law professors. One afternoon, Judge Alexander told his protégé why he made the decision to stand up and resist the Ku Klux Klan:

> It's the Constitution, Leon, the foundation of our country. The men who worked so long and so hard to produce such an invincible doctrine were, in my belief, God-inspired. For it is one doctrine that can weather any controversy, any argument put against it by man.
>
> There will always be those who will try to go around it because it doesn't fit their individual goals—even though in their minds their aims are for the good of the state or mankind.
>
> Take that man who was tarred and feathered. It could well be that he was immoral. But the moment the Klan

2. Jaworski, *Crossroads* (Elgin, IL: David C. Cook Publishing, 1981), 43.

picked him up outside the law, you, I, and every other citizen was [*sic*] in mortal danger.

Perhaps someday people may feel that a judge who decides against joining such an organization is an enemy of the country. Perhaps they may decide that anyone with a foreign-sounding name is suspect.

Against this we have only one defense, next to God, and that is the United States Constitution. God help us, if anyone in authority ever tries to subvert it.[3]

Taking those words to heart, nineteen-year-old Leon Jaworski, soon to become the youngest person ever admitted to the State Bar of Texas, made this pledge: "I vowed to do everything I could to become the kind of lawyer [James P. Alexander] was."[4]

And so he did.

In *Crossroads*, published one year before his death, Jaworski devoted chapters to the five cases he regarded as the most important in his life. All had a connection to his law school vow, all took place in the criminal arena, and in all of them, a self-described "muffin-faced" lawyer raised the bar to new heights of professionalism and protected the Rule of Law.

STATE OF TEXAS V. JORDAN SCOTT

In 1929, when Harper Lee was only three years old, Leon Jaworski got the chance to be Atticus Finch in real life. Waco criminal district judge Richard Munroe appointed Leon Jaworski (age twenty-three at the time) to represent Jordan Scott, an African American defendant accused of murdering a Caucasian couple. Like Mr. Finch, the young lawyer faced a stacked deck in defending his black client (who professed his innocence in private to Jaworski and in his courtroom testimony)—who had allegedly committed a felony against white persons—at a trial to be conducted before an all-white, all-male small-town jury in a racially prejudiced community. The public's obsession with the case became so extreme that both

---

3. Ibid., 44.

4. Ibid., 43.

Jaworski and his client faced death threats. At the end of the trial, the jury convicted Mr. Scott, largely due to his involuntary confession and its being inflamed by the district attorney's closing argument, during which he railed against "this colored Negro, this brute, this assassin!"

Despite the adverse verdict, Jaworski achieved more justice for Jordan Scott than Atticus Finch did for Tom Robinson, persuading Judge Munroe that his client deserved a new trial due to the coerced confession and the prosecutor's inflammatory statements. The procedural victory proved to be short lived, however, when before the second trial started, Mr. Scott confided to his lawyer (for the first time) that he, in fact, had killed the white couple. At the second trial, Jaworski still vigorously defended his client, but again the jury came back with a guilty verdict, which stood up on appeal, and Jordan Scott ended his life in the electric chair.

In *Crossroads*, Jaworski consoled himself over the outcome of the Scott case, knowing he had fulfilled his duty to his client and the profession:

> I had defended Scott to the best of my ability. Even if I had known of his guilt from the beginning, my responsibilities would have been discharged in exactly the same manner. The prosecution for the state still would have had to discharge its burden—that of proving him guilty beyond a reasonable doubt.
>
> The entire process was a grueling experience for me, but I was sustained by the feeling that I had contributed to the undergirding of our system of justice by protecting the rights of every defendant, even one guilty of a dastardly crime.[5]

---

5. Ibid., 58.

PROSECUTION OF NAZI WAR CRIMINALS
DURING AND AFTER WORLD WAR II

In his mid-thirties, shortly after the attack on Pearl Harbor, Jaworski left behind in Houston his wife, three preadolescent children, and a growing law firm to join the office of the judge advocate general, where he would ultimately prosecute German war criminals in Camp Chaffee, Arkansas (1943–1944); Paris, France (early 1945); Wiesbaden, Germany (after V-E Day in May 1945); Hadamar, Germany (early October 1945); and Dachau, Germany (later in October 1945). Before Jaworski's release from the army, Brigadier General Edward C. Betts and the JAG War Crimes Department presented the forty-year-old colonel with the Legion of Merit award for his meritorious service.

His wartime experience made such a deep impression that Jaworski later wrote a book about it, *After Fifteen Years*, with a foreword by his friend, client, and then vice president of the United States, Lyndon B. Johnson. The book's theme is Jaworski's struggle to grasp how so many once-virtuous and religious German people managed to lose their moral compass, follow orders from the madman Hitler, and repeatedly engage in unconscionable acts of homicide. The lawyer offered this conclusion on what had caused the Germans to compromise their righteousness:

> They remained silent when opposition should have been sounded. They ignored the admonition of Edmund Burke that, "All that is necessary for the forces of evil to win this world is for enough good men to do nothing."
> . . .
>
> Any nation, once permitting the cancerous growth of evil and depravity to gain hold, will find her moral sinew destroyed eventually, and when it is gone, only ruination can take its place.[6]

Jaworski then refined that conclusion twenty years later in his final book, *Crossroads*:

---

6. Jaworski, *After Fifteen Years*, (Houston, TX: Gulf Publishing Company, 1961), 12–13.

A seed of evil always seems to be within us, waiting for that unguarded moment to take over.

I remembered all of [the Nazi Germans] I had met in the past months who had allowed that seed to grow through callousness, or fear of not belonging, to where it eventually consumed them and their nation.[7]

Jaworski's postwar reflections on the experience of prosecuting Nazis in his book published in 1961 foreshadowed his actions and reflections twelve years later in dealing with the Watergate conspirators, who also at one time had been honorable men but chose to "remain silent when opposition should have been sounded" and "in unguarded moments allowed the seed of evil to take over and consume them," and therefore also committed crimes at the behest of another manipulative leader. In his 1961 book, the lawyer-author questioned whether what he had witnessed in Germany during the mid-1940s could ever happen in the United States, and he gave this ominous answer using 20/20 foresight:

No nation, no matter how powerful and great and whatever be its form of government, can long withstand the stranglehold of moral deterioration in its people.

How then is this deterioration to be averted? Again, the answer today is the answer of fifteen years ago. The free institutions that made America great must be kept strong and effective, and their work, done faithfully and militantly under God and the Constitution, will preserve us.

Those who were tortured and died on the streets of Russelsheim, in the blighted halls of Hadamar, and in the gas chambers of Dachau will have served mankind well after all, if these truths of freedom survive because of them.

---

7. Jaworski, *Crossroads*, 118.

And, after fifteen years, this is the lesson I have had welling up in me—to be passed on to as many of my fellow freemen as have read this recollection of a lifetime.[8]

Unfortunately, Richard Nixon and his band of yes-men advisers apparently never read Leon Jaworski's book and therefore did not absorb the lessons on moral deterioration of Russelsheim, Hadamar, and Dachau. The rest is history.

STATE OF TEXAS V. RON COOPER

Immediately after the Texas Court of Criminal Appeals issued an opinion in 1958 affirming the trial court's conviction of Ron Cooper for the murder of his mother-in-law, Leon Jaworski was confronted by the plea of his minister, Charles King, to turn things around due to the injustice of Mr. Cooper's facing the electric chair when he obviously lacked mental capacity at the time he committed the crime—his incapacity being so clear it had earlier led to his discharge from the army. At first, Jaworski responded to his pastor's request by trying to beg off from what appeared to be the impossible task of reversing a judgment after it had already been affirmed by the highest available appellate court. His minister, however, would not take no for an answer and implored his good friend and parishioner to perform a legal miracle, using words the lawyer could not ignore: "Well, Leon, it is between you and the Lord."[9]

The deeply religious Jaworski could not escape his conscience and would not disappoint his preacher, so he took the case. In short order, he obtained an extension of time to file a motion for rehearing with the Court of Criminal Appeals; then he filed the motion; then he lost the motion on a 2-1 decision; then he filed a second motion for rehearing (allowable only because he had obtained a dissent in the first motion's disposition); and then he won the second motion for rehearing 2-1, earning the right to a new trial. Before the new trial commenced, the state's expert witness psychiatrist and the district attorney both acknowledged they had erred in their earlier assess-

---

8. Jaworski, *After Fifteen Years*, 153–154.

9. Jaworski, *Crossroads*, 133.

ment of the defendant's mental capacity, and, at a subsequent sanity hearing, a new psychiatrist evaluated Cooper's condition and determined that the army's conclusion had been correct as to his incapacity, meaning he was unfit to stand trial.

Instead of being executed, Ron Cooper got to live out the rest of his days in a mental institution, as Leon Jaworski had found a way to save his client's life just as the state was warming up the electric chair.

In *Crossroads*, Jaworski reflected on the miracle that spared the life of Ron Cooper:

> I firmly believe it was a case, pure and simple, of the influence of God's Holy Spirit. By being obedient to him, my role was merely that of an instrument.
>
> Thus, in contrast to the vengeful atmosphere of the first trial, the authorities were impelled to be Christlike in justice, patience, and compassion. In the end, they applied the judicial process of the United States Constitution as it was meant to operate.[10]

Although the cases of Jordan Scott, the Nazi war criminals, and Ron Cooper earned Leon Jaworski precious little in the way of fees, they fulfilled the lawyer's highest responsibility to his profession in every matter handled, regardless of its profitability. Jaworski expressed as much in his lectures on the subject, "The Lawyer in Society," given at Baylor University Law School in September 1980:

> The greatest reward that flows to a lawyer is not measured in riches, social position, or popularity. Rather, it comes as an unseen, intangible inner satisfaction that emanates from the faithful discharge of duty. This is truly the lawyer's highest form of compensation.[11]

UNITED STATES V. ROSS BARNETT

In September 1962, after serving nine years in the U.S. Air Force, a twenty-nine-year-old African American named James Meredith

10. Ibid., 138.

11. Jaworski, *The Lawyer in Society* (Waco, TX: Baylor University Press, 2007), 31.

prepared to become the trailblazer who would integrate the University of Mississippi. Before the fall semester began, Mr. Meredith's road to higher education in Oxford appeared clear since the U.S. Fifth Circuit Court of Appeals had just ordered the State of Mississippi to allow him to enroll at Ole Miss.

Amazingly, Mississippi governor Ross Barnett believed he had the authority to disregard the Fifth Circuit's ruling and refused admittance to Meredith, claiming that his state's rights trumped the federal court's order. After U.S. Attorney General Robert Kennedy participated in a series of phone conversations with Barnett, unsuccessfully seeking to persuade the governor to reconsider his decision, Kennedy knew criminal contempt proceedings against Barnett had to be pursued, but due to his many phone conversations, he believed he would be a witness in any future litigation. Because of that circumstance, the attorney general asked Leon Jaworski to serve as the Justice Department's special litigation counsel and specifically directed the Houston lawyer (who at the time was serving as president of the State Bar of Texas) to take all necessary action within the law to bring Barnett into compliance with the Fifth Circuit's ruling.

When Kennedy offered him the Barnett assignment, Jaworski regarded what was happening in Mississippi as "the most serious confrontation between state and federal authorities since the Civil War."[12] Led by its defiant governor, the state was in the midst of full-blown rebellion marked by its citizens firing guns and throwing rocks at the U.S. troops and marshals stationed in Oxford to protect Meredith and regain a semblance of order. Dissidents and local politicians filled the airwaves advocating secession.

Weighing whether to accept the attorney general's offer, Jaworski saw on television the rampant disregard for law around Ole Miss, and it reminded him of the Nazi hoodlums who had looted Jewish homes and shops two decades before. Finally, he agreed to assist the Justice Department and do what it took to obtain enforcement of the Fifth Circuit's order against Governor Barnett, regardless of how unpopular it would make him in Texas. In *Crossroads*, he explained why he made his difficult decision:

---

12. Jaworski, *Crossroads*, 141.

I would have to live in reality. I would have to face the fact that my roots were in Texas, a state very much a part of the South.

Yet I knew that Southern tradition must have no part in my decision. Mine had to be based on the law of our country. Moreover, if court decrees are to be flouted, there soon would be no law—in the South or elsewhere.[13]

Jaworski's law partner, Gibson Gayle, would later say, "All Bobby Kennedy had to do to get Jaworski to say yes was tell him, 'Leon, your country needs you.'"[14]

In a statement that would synchronize with his assessment of the central figure in a subsequent legal assignment (as Watergate special prosecutor) a decade later, Jaworski said of Ross Barnett,

If a United States citizen was allowed to choose which laws or court orders to obey and which to defy, it could erode our system of government. . . . If we do nothing about such defiances, they will certainly escalate and soon the rule of law will have lost its force and the rights and liberties of all of us will be imperiled.[15]

Just as Atticus Finch became unpopular in Maycomb, Alabama, among many in the white community for his zealous representation of Tom Robinson, Leon Jaworski received major hostility throughout Houston for his efforts to bring Governor Barnett to justice for defying a federal appellate court's order. Local police had to stand guard at Jaworski's home, major clients threatened to take business from his law firm, crank calls poured into his home and office day and night, social friends turned their backs on him at parties and sporting events, and Jaworski even considered resigning as state bar president because of the massive controversy surrounding him.

Despite such virulent antagonism, Leon Jaworski stayed on task, pursuing Barnett for two years, prevailing in hearings on behalf of the Department of Justice before the Fifth Circuit and the U.S. Su-

---

13. Ibid., 149.

14. Gibson Gayle, personal communication to author, June 28, 2011.

15. Jaworski, *Crossroads*, 152.

preme Court. By 1964, Barnett's term as governor had ended, James Meredith had gained traction as a student at Ole Miss, and Robert Kennedy had stepped down as attorney general after his brother's assassination. These circumstances culminated in the Justice Department's decision to dismiss the contempt proceeding against Barnett, since the points at issue had essentially become moot.

In his autobiography, *Confession and Avoidance*, Jaworski reflected on the import of his work in pursuing Ross Barnett. He noted that if criminal contempt proceedings had not been brought against the governor for his defiance of court orders, "others very likely would have been encouraged to follow his foolhardy example, the Rule of Law would have been weakened, and the struggle for equal rights made more difficult, and bloodier."[16]

UNITED STATES V. NIXON

In 1968 and 1972, Leon Jaworski, who until then had spent his adult life supporting political candidates of the Democratic Party, voted for a Republican, Richard Nixon, in the presidential election. As news reports hit the airwaves on June 17, 1972, of the burglary at the Democratic National Committee headquarters in the Watergate complex in Washington, DC, Jaworski assumed a few overzealous campaign workers had exercised bad judgment, and after they got their wrists slapped over the attempted theft, the incident would soon go away without disturbing President Nixon's popularity. At first, it appeared that that might be the case. In November 1972, the incumbent president won the electoral votes of every state except one (Massachusetts), thereby prevailing in one of the biggest presidential election landslide victories in American history.

As Congress's, the media's, and the FBI's investigations of the break-in progressed, however, evidence began to reveal that the burglars had not acted alone but had been directed by their campaign superiors, some of whom had connections that extended into the Justice Department and perhaps even the Oval Office.

When Attorney General Richard Kleindienst resigned April 30,

16. Jaworski, *Confession and Avoidance* (New York: Doubleday, 1979), 170.

1973, after acknowledging his failure to disclose his meeting with Watergate conspirator G. Gordon Liddy shortly after the break-in (where Liddy requested Kleindienst's assistance in getting burglar James McCord released from jail), the president nominated Elliot Richardson as Kleindienst's successor. Feeling distrustful toward any Nixon nominee, even someone as squeaky clean as Richardson, the Senate refused to confirm the new nominee for attorney general unless Nixon agreed to appoint an outside special prosecutor, who would act independent of the Justice Department, to pursue the Watergate investigation. With no real choice, following Richardson's confirmation, President Nixon allowed his new attorney general to appoint Harvard Law School professor (and President Kennedy's solicitor general) Archibald Cox to serve as Watergate special prosecutor beginning in May 1973. Richardson immediately gave Cox carte blanche authority to assemble a legal team to fully investigate the case and prosecute any and all wrongdoers.

On May 17, 1973, a Senate Select Committee chaired by Senator Sam Ervin commenced its own investigation of the Watergate break-in and coverup. Almost two months later, in giving a background interview to lawyers working for Ervin's committee, Deputy Assistant Alexander Butterfield disclosed for the first time that all conversations in the Oval Office during 1972 and 1973 had been taped. Soon thereafter, Butterfield publicly confirmed the tapes' existence in his testimony before Ervin's committee.

On July 17, Senator Ervin wrote Nixon a letter requesting turnover of the tapes, and a day later, Special Prosecutor Archibald Cox did the same. The president refused to produce them, per his letter of July 23 to Ervin and Nixon lawyer Charles Alan Wright's letter of the same date to Cox. Upon receiving Wright's letter, Cox immediately went to U.S. district judge John Sirica in Washington, DC (the chief judge of the district court overseeing the grand jury investigating obstructions of justice and other crimes committed by persons in the Nixon administration and the Committee to Re-elect the President), and obtained issuance of a subpoena duces tecum requiring the production of nine specifically identified tapes (though there were sixty-four other tapes that were not subpoenaed at that time). After the subpoena was served on White House counsel Fred Buzhardt, Nixon announced he would not obey it, causing Cox to move for a show cause order, which Judge Sirica granted, setting a hearing for the president to demonstrate why he should not be required to produce the tapes.

Battles over the nine tapes continued into October. On October 19, President Nixon sent a letter to Cox instructing him to stop attempting to obtain tapes, notes, or memoranda of presidential conversation by means of judicial process. The Watergate special prosecutor replied by going public that evening to the *Washington Star* newspaper, stating that he felt the president was refusing to comply with the court and that Nixon's order to stop requesting materials was in violation of the promises that the attorney general had made to the Senate. The next day, October 20, Cox held a news conference at the National Press Club, in which he stressed that he was not "out to get" the president but he was merely trying to do his duty as special prosecutor, which involved bringing to the court's attention what appeared to be Nixon's noncompliance with the court's order.

Cox then proceeded to reject Nixon's settlement offer of producing typed transcripts of the tapes prepared (and surely edited) by the president's staff and which would supposedly be verified as accurate by Senator John Stennis, in lieu of getting the chance to listen to the actual tapes themselves. A few hours later, at the president's direction, Archibald Cox got fired by solicitor general Robert Bork, serving as acting attorney general, after both Elliot Richardson and deputy attorney general William Ruckelshaus refused to terminate Cox.[17] The chain of events became known as the "Saturday Night Massacre" and ended with White House press secretary Ron Ziegler's announcing to the public that the Watergate Special Prosecution Force had been abolished around eight o'clock that night.

Fortunately, before the Massacre took place, Cox's legal team had taken precautions to protect their files, fearing that all their hard work to date might be destroyed by a regiment of Nixon's thugs. British journalist Fred Emery covered the Watergate story for the *London Times*, and in his book *Watergate* reported that many Ameri-

---

17. Richardson resigned from his post and Ruckelshaus was fired.

cans responded to the Massacre with the fear that they were either in the midst of a military coup similar to the events in the recent best-selling novel *Seven Days in May* or else sensed "there was a whiff of the Gestapo in the chill October air."[18]

The public, the Congress (both Democrats and Republicans), the media, and the American Bar Association all expressed total outrage over the Massacre and in unison asserted that the time had come for impeachment proceedings to begin. The House Judiciary Committee, chaired by New Jersey congressman Peter Rodino, began scheduling hearings to determine whether impeachment was appropriate.

In response to the Massacre, Judge John Sirica called into his courtroom the grand juries charged with investigating obstructions of justice and other federal crimes related to Nixon and his people and assured them and the remaining members of the special prosecutor's legal team that regardless of the firing and resignations, they were to press on with their duties.

Three days after the Massacre, the compliance date arrived for production of the nine tapes under Judge Sirica's order (that had just been affirmed by the DC Circuit Court of Appeals), and to the surprise of the special prosecution team and the media, the president's lawyer, Charles Alan Wright, announced to the court that his client would comply with the order. Soon, when the subpoenaed tapes were produced, major skepticism about the credibility of the production arose when the president claimed that two of the nine tapes he had agreed to deliver under the subpoena now mysteriously did not exist because of an alleged failure to tape two key meetings. Furthermore, the June 20 tape, one of the seven actually produced by Nixon, contained an eighteen-minute erased gap.

As the Watergate special prosecution legal team carried on (without Cox) at Sirica's direction (despite the fact that Acting Attorney General Robert Bork had purportedly abolished the Special Prosecutor's Office on October 23 and announced that the Watergate investigation would be continued by the Justice Department), in an attempt to slow Congress's impeachment momentum, Nixon de-

---

18. Fred Emery, *Watergate: The Corruption of American Politics and the Fall of Richard Nixon* (New York: Random House, 1994), 401.

cided he'd have to name a successor to Cox, and he selected Leon Jaworski as the man.

Why Leon Jaworski? In President Nixon's memoirs, *RN*, he gave the following explanation for why Jaworski was chosen to succeed Archibald Cox as Watergate special prosecutor:

> Robert Bork, as Acting Attorney General, began searching for a new Special Prosecutor. A few days later, [Chief of Staff Alexander] Haig reported to me that he and Bork had concluded that Leon Jaworski, a successful Houston lawyer, a former president of the American Bar Association, and a prominent Texas Democrat, was the right man for the job. Haig had already tentatively approached Jaworski, who had said he would accept if he could have our agreement that in the event we came to an impasse he could sue me in the courts for evidence. I agreed to this condition, and, as a further guarantee, we announced that there would have to be a supportive consensus of the Majority and Minority Leaders of the House and Senate and the ranking majority and minority members of the House and Senate Judiciary Committees before he could be fired.
>
> Within ten days of the Cox firing and after the high political price I had had to pay for ridding myself of him, I was back in the same trap of having to accept a Watergate Special Prosecutor. But there was one major difference: I had been told that, unlike Cox, Jaworski would be fair and objective. Although as a Democrat he would be under pressure from other Democrats to score partisan points, I was led to believe that he respected the office of the presidency and that therefore he would not mount court challenges just for the plaudits and publicity he would thereby receive. Haig said that Jaworski recognized that the staff assembled by Cox was excessively anti-Nixon and that he was determined not to become their captive. He told Haig that he planned to bring in his own people and would see to it that the staff limited its

activity to relevant and proper areas. Haig liked Jaworski and was impressed by him; he told me that Jaworski would be a tough prosecutor but not a partisan who was simply out to get me.[19]

In his Watergate memoir, *The Right and the Power*, Jaworski said he believed Haig wanted him as Cox's successor because of having been assured by others that "this guy won't be out after the President's scalp."[20] When the Houston lawyer arrived at the White House and received strong assurances from Haig of having unrestricted independence if he accepted the job, Jaworski listened as Haig pulled out all stops to persuade him to take the position, using the same type of plea to enlist his service as Robert Kennedy had used on him in 1962:

> I'm putting the patriotic monkey on your back, Mr. Jaworski. The situation in this country is almost revolutionary. Things are about to come apart. The only hope of stabilizing the situation is for the President to be able to announce that someone in whom the country has confidence has agreed to serve.[21]

The patriotic call to duty worked. Sixty-eight-year-old Leon Jaworski took the job.

From the time Jaworski became Watergate special prosecutor on November 5, 1973, until he resigned effective October 25, 1974, he engaged in an extended series of shrewd tactics and made prudent decisions that allowed him to achieve his goal of pursuing all the evidence necessary to get to the truth. The most notable of these tactics and decisions were the following:

- To the surprise of many, Jaworski chose to retain all of Cox's team of hard-charging lawyers. These thirty-seven attorneys, average age thirty-one, would perform the heavy preparation lifting and would ultimately try the cases, while their boss did

---

19. Nixon, *RN* (New York: Grosset & Dunlap, 1978), 943–944.

20. Jaworski, *The Right and the Power* (Houston, TX: Gulf Publishing, 1976), 4.

21. Ibid.

the heavy thinking and called the final shots on the toughest decisions. More than anyone else, President Nixon had hoped Jaworski would release Cox's aggressive group and recruit his own lawyers, thereby necessitating the start of a whole new learning curve, which would substantially delay the investigation and prosecution. Jaworski could see that Cox's very capable young prosecutors had the train on the tracks and it was gaining speed. Why alter that? If it ain't broke, don't fix it. Cox's team's initial doubts about whether their new boss would get them to the goal line were soon erased by the tenacious, direct, and pragmatic Jaworski, who seized each day with steadfast focus on the task at hand and showed genuine respect for his new colleagues' opinions and skills. They quickly saw the truth in what Jaworski told *Time* magazine after he became Watergate special prosecutor: "At my stage of life, do you think I would come in here and be part of anything that would ruin whatever name and reputation I have established over the years?"[22]

- Upon assuming his duties as Watergate special prosecutor, Jaworski expressed full support of the aggressive inquiry being made by the assistant prosecutors to find out the cause of the eighteen-minute gap on the June 20 tape in the week following the Massacre, thereby sending the immediate message to his lawyer team, the media, and the public that he planned to pick up exactly where Cox had left off.

- From the first time his name appeared on a pleading in his new position (in working on the reply brief to Egil Krogh's motion to dismiss perjury), Jaworski pulled no punches in his perception of what Nixon and his cohorts were attempting to do:

> No government office, not even the highest office in the land, carries with it the right to ignore the law's command. . . . While the claim of national security gives these claims of legalized burglary and perjury

---

22. "Charging Nixon's Men," *Time*, March 11, 1974, 12.

a deceptively compelling ring, ultimately they rest on
a wholesale rejection of the rule of law.[23]

He would make this unvarnished "in your face" argument in
every motion and brief he filed and each oral argument he
made to a court until Richard Nixon resigned.

- In December 1973, when Jaworski first heard the March 21,
  1973, tape (on which Nixon clearly coached his lieutenants on
  how to avoid telling the truth in their testimony), the special
  prosecutor knew that the president (not his lieutenants,
  but the president!) had encouraged and authorized perjury
  and the payment of hush money to the Watergate burglars.
  Therefore, Nixon had definitely participated in the crime of
  conspiracy to obstruct justice, and at some point, his criminal
  activity would have to be addressed. What was a consummate
  professional and American patriot to do in this unique
  situation where he knew the president of the United States
  had broken the law yet had surrounded himself with only yes-
  men civil lawyers? Jaworski immediately met with Chief of
  Staff Haig and told him the president quickly needed to retain
  the best criminal defense lawyer he could find. Haig heard
  the advice and denied that there was any need for such, but
  soon thereafter Nixon hired Boston criminal defense attorney
  James St. Clair.

- As the president kept trying new ways to avoid producing
  the remaining sixty-four tapes requested by Jaworski, such
  avoidance techniques ranging from Nixon's offering the
  special prosecutor his own edited (i.e., misrepresented)
  versions of transcripts to his agreeing to answer all questions
  by responding to written interrogatories, Jaworski saw
  through each of the president's ruses and wouldn't stop until
  he had the real thing.

- During his months as Watergate special prosecutor, Jaworski
  rejected Nixon's many offers to meet face-to-face to discuss
  resolution, believing such a meeting could have no upside and

23. Jaworski, *The Right and the Power*, 23.

would definitely have the downside of his losing credibility with his own special prosecution team, the media, and the public.

- As Peter Rodino's House Judiciary Committee pursued its own Watergate investigation on the road to impeachment, Special Prosecutor Jaworski found himself on unplowed ground. How best to get the fruits of the grand jury's confidential work product into the hands of Rodino's committee in a lawful manner in a high-stakes scenario where there was no legal precedent to guide them? Jaworski and his legal team devised a strategy of preparing an objective and detailed "road map" report that gave the complete chronology of every material fact in the burglary and subsequent coverup, and it was supported by the hard evidence tied to each entry in the timeline, which included the most compelling parts of the seven tapes Nixon had previously produced. On March 1, 1974, Jaworski and his team delivered to Judge Sirica the indictments of Mitchell, Haldeman, Ehrlichman, et al., and with them also delivered the road map report in a sealed envelope along with a "bulging briefcase" (filled with the backup to support the report). Upon receiving them, in his discretion pursuant to the Federal Rules of Criminal Procedure, the judge turned the report and briefcase over to Rodino's committee so its learning curve could be expedited and they could avoid duplicating what the Watergate special prosecutor and grand jury had already done. Conspirators H. R. Haldeman and Gordon Strachan appealed Judge Sirica's decision to deliver the report and briefcase to the grand jury, but the DC Circuit Court of Appeals affirmed Sirica's execution of the special prosecutor's plan, and the losing parties did not attempt to take the issue up with the Supreme Court.

- Though Jaworski knew long before getting the remaining sixty-four tapes that he probably had enough evidence to persuade the grand jury to indict Nixon, there were legal issues in play that had never been addressed before in considering such an option. For instance, there was a question as to whether a president could be subjected to a criminal indictment while in office. Jaworski therefore determined that they should instead pursue impeachment. Another issue that arose was that of characterizing Nixon's role. Richard Ben-Veniste, among the top young lawyers working under Jaworski in the Watergate Special Prosecutor's Office, noted in his book *The Emperor's New Clothes* (New York: St. Martin's Press, 2009), that prosecutors typically identify unindicted co-conspirators either in the body of the indictment or in a later "bill of particulars" filed before trial. Jaworski, however, became convinced that this should be left to Congress, once it reviewed the evidence supporting impeachment.

- For evidentiary purposes, to have full use of all relevant evidence (including the tapes) in prosecuting the other co-conspirators (besides Nixon) who had obstructed justice, Jaworski accepted the suggestion offered by Ben-Veniste and got the grand jury to cast their votes for all who they believed to be unindicted co-conspirators. They then voted for Nixon and listed him with the others in a confidential bill of particulars that would not be made a matter of public record but would be read to and used by Judge Sirica later to allow all evidence of the conspiracy to come in against all the defendants being prosecuted. With this approach, all the tapes became admissible in all the trials, and Jaworski avoided public disclosure of the fact that President Nixon was regarded not only by the special prosecutor but also by the grand jury as a co-conspirator. With no such public disclosure of the grand jury's assessment, there could be no claim of Jaworski's team having caused any prejudice against Nixon while the House Judiciary Committee considered impeachment.

- After months of fruitless discussions and letter exchanges on the subject of Nixon's producing the remaining sixty-four tapes voluntarily, Jaworski decided that the time had come to play hardball. On April 16, 1974, he obtained a subpoena that required Nixon to produce the tapes.

- After Judge Sirica denied the president's motion to quash subpoena, St. Clair immediately appealed Sirica's ruling to the DC Circuit Court of Appeals. Jaworski knew that regardless of how the DC Circuit ruled on the subpoena enforceability issue, the case would definitely end up at the Supreme Court. He also knew the Supreme Court would soon be adjourning for its summer recess, and going through the briefing and oral argument process with the DC Circuit would cause enough delay that the case wouldn't be reached by the Supreme Court until after its summer recess. How to avoid this delay? Jaworski expedited the appellate disposition by invoking a rarely used federal court procedural option that could allow him to bypass the circuit court of appeals and go straight to the Supreme Court. Jaworski correctly believed that the subpoena enforcement case fit within the criteria allowing such a direct appeal to the Supreme Court because it satisfied the criteria of having "imperative public importance as to require immediate settlement."[24] Jaworski's procedural gamble worked. The Supreme Court agreed that the DC Circuit Court of Appeals could be skipped over, granted writ of certiorari, and scheduled oral argument for July 8, 1974. The sole issue Jaworski framed in his brief to the Supreme Court was the following:

  > Whether the President, in a pending prosecution against his former aides and associates being conducted in the name of the United States by a Special Prosecutor not subject to Presidential directions, may withhold material evidence from the Court merely on his assertion that the evidence involves confidential government deliberations.[25]

- Though Leon Jaworski spent most of his career as a trial lawyer, he had also earned high ranking officer stripes as an appellate lawyer. He addressed the U.S. Supreme Court for sixty minutes

---

24. Jaworski, *The Right and the Power*, 148.

25. Ibid., 170.

on July 8 and had ready answers to the questions with which they interrupted him 115 times. Jaworski would later say of his oral argument, "It was obvious the Justices were not in the frame of mind for oratory. They wanted facts and the truths on which they rested."[26] Never before *United States v. Nixon* had the Supreme Court considered the scope of executive privilege. Jaworski's argument focused on certain questions, including, "Who is to be the arbiter of what the Constitution says?" He noted that Nixon had invoked provisions of the Constitution in refusing to produce evidence, but the president's reading of the Constitution might not necessarily be correct. "If he is wrong, who is there to tell him so? And if there is no one, then the President, of course, is free to pursue his course of erroneous interpretations. What then becomes of our constitutional form of government?" Jaworski then provided this answer to those questions: "This nation's constitutional form of government is in serious jeopardy if the President, any President, is to say that the Constitution means what he says it does, and that there is no one, not even the Supreme Court, to tell him otherwise."[27]

- When the Supreme Court released its unanimous opinion on July 24, 1974, affirming Judge Sirica's ruling and holding that the subpoena should be enforced (and therefore requiring President Nixon to produce the remaining tapes), the Court did not provide a timetable for the tapes' delivery. Despite his exhilaration over the Supreme Court's decision, Jaworski wasted no time and the next day went before Judge Sirica to obtain a definite timetable for the production of the tapes. At the judge's request, the parties negotiated between themselves and soon reached an agreement for the timing of the production. On August 5, 1974, the president produced the tapes, including the fateful June 23, 1972, tape on which Nixon told Ehrlichman to direct the CIA's deputy director to have the FBI stop its investigation of the hush money paid

---

26. Ibid., 193.
27. Ibid., 194.

to the Watergate burglars. This June 23 tape established once and for all, contrary to his past denials, that Nixon had started obstructing justice only six days after the Watergate burglary. Proven by his own voice in the tapes to be both a professed prevaricator (or in Nixon's words, the new tapes were "at variance with my previous statements") and a full-blown obstructer of justice, and knowing that the prospects for impeachment had gone from possible to certain, on August 8, 1974, Richard Nixon resigned as president of the United States.

• After Gerald Ford was sworn in, the most pressing question for the new president became whether he would allow Jaworski and his team to press on and have the grand jury indict private citizen Richard Nixon. As Ford evaluated what to do, he asked Jaworski's opinion on how long it would be before Nixon could be given a fair trial, if he were in-dicted. Jaworski pointed out various difficulties and noted the uniqueness of the situation, indicating that the time needed to obtain a fair trial would be hard to estimate. On September 8, 1974, to get the country to move on and be-cause of his concern over whether his predecessor could receive a fair trial, President Ford (a lawyer) pardoned Richard Nixon. Immediately, many members of Congress, law pro-fessors, and the media challenged Jaworski to litigate the con-stitutionality of the pardon, but after reviewing pertinent authorities, Jaworski determined that such a challenge would be frivolous since the new president had clearly acted within his rights.

• For his last hurrah, Jaworski organized his assistant special prosecutors to try Ehrlichman, Haldeman, Mitchell, et al. in trials that commenced October 1, 1974, and resulted in "all the president's men" being convicted over the next three months. Jaworski decided he didn't need to participate in the trials, knowing his legal team was more than up to the job. On October 25, 1974, he resigned from his duties as Watergate special prosecutor, returned home to Houston, and rejoined his law firm.

In his last book, *Crossroads*, Leon Jaworski said that as a teenager, "encouraged by my success [as a high school debater], and attracted by the challenge of defending the rights of others in a free society, I decided to become a lawyer."[28]

Upon reaching that goal, Jaworski proceeded to defend the rights of his many clients, including those in his most notable cases: Jordan Scott, the U.S. Army and Nazi war crime victims, Ron Cooper, the Department of Justice and federal court system in the face of Ross Barnett's defiance, and the American people in confronting Richard Nixon's quest to put himself above the law.

Those who knew him best knew that Leon Jaworski never aspired to be famous. As proof of this, his friends noted that, early in his career, he had turned down the opportunity offered by Governor Beauford Jester shortly after World War II to serve on the Texas Supreme Court, and he later spurned President Lyndon Johnson's overtures to be nominated for the U.S. Supreme Court. In addition to that, without Jaworski's ever intentionally seeking to lead the Houston Bar Association, the American College of Trial Lawyers, the State Bar of Texas, or the American Bar Association, his colleagues virtually elevated him by acclamation to become president of all four organizations.

On the subject of pursuing fame, Jaworski as a young man had read and remembered the words of British poet Alexander Pope:

> Unblemished, let me live and die unknown.
> Give me an honest fame or give me none.

At the time of his death in 1982, Leon Jaworski had answered Pope's call to live life "unblemished" and earn only an "honest fame" in his fifty-seven-year career as a consummate lawyer. His impact in righting wrongs and preserving the Rule of Law culminated with his achievement as the Watergate special prosecutor in 1974, when he preserved the Constitution as the Supreme Law of the Land and succeeded in enforcing its system of checks and balances. Jaworski

---

28. Jaworski, *Crossroads*, 30.

concluded his Watergate memoirs, *The Right and the Power*, with these words that summarize his ultimate triumph in "raising the bar":

> From Watergate we learned what generations before us have known: our Constitution works. And during the Watergate years it was interpreted again so as to reaffirm that no one—absolutely no one—is above the law.[29]

JAMES A. BAKER, III

> The case for pragmatic idealism is based on an optimistic view of man, tempered by our knowledge of human imperfection. It promises no easy answers or quick fixes. But I am convinced that it offers our surest guide and best hope for navigating our great country safely through this precarious period of opportunity and risk in world affairs.[30]

In their historic careers, Leon Jaworski and James A. Baker, III, ended up in the same place—the highest level of achievement in their respective fields as lawyers—though they didn't start from the same place. Leonidas Jaworski entered the world in 1905 as the son of Joseph Jaworski, a German-speaking Polish immigrant, who went through Ellis Island two years before Leon's birth and made a modest living as an evangelical pastor leading small churches in Central Texas towns.

James A. Baker, III, entered the world in 1930 as the son, grandson, and great-grandson of distinguished lawyers all named James A. Baker,[31] who each made a good living working at the Baker Botts law firm (formed by Baker's great-grandfather) in Houston.

Rising from a humble beginning, Leon Jaworski took his in-

---

29. Jaworski, *The Right and the Power*, 279.

30. James Baker, *Work Hard, Study . . . and Keep out of Politics!*, rev. ed. (Evanston, IL: Northwestern University Press, 2008), 447.

31. In a footnote to his autobiography, *Work Hard, Study . . . and Keep out of Politics!* (New York: G. P. Putnam's Sons, 2006), James A. Baker, III, explains that although he's actually the fourth generation to bear the name, "the numbering didn't start until I came along" (12).

terrogation, advocacy, and passion-for-justice talents as far as they could go, making an impact all the way from Europe (in prosecuting Nazi war criminals) to the U.S. Supreme Court. Rising from a comfortable beginning, James A. Baker, III (hereinafter identified in this chapter as "James Baker"), took his counseling, negotiating, and deal-making talents as far as they could go, making an impact all the way from the White House; to the Commerce, Treasury, and State departments; to the United Nations and around the world.

THE HOUSTON YEARS

When James Baker left the University of Texas Law School in 1957, he believed the only real lawyers were trial lawyers. With that perspective, after passing the bar exam, he spent his first two years doing civil litigation as an associate at the Houston law firm of Andrews, Kurth, Campbell & Bradley.[32] Soon he learned what Leon Jaworski and every other litigator comes to know: people often lie under oath.

As the fourth in a generational string of eminent lawyers, James Baker had grown up respecting the work of those whose name he bore as well as the profession he had chosen for himself, and he recoiled at the idea of spending his career attempting to win trials where witness perjury appeared to be more the rule than the exception.

What to do? In his book *The Politics of Diplomacy*, James Baker explained that in looking for a plan B after rejecting litigation, he sought "a good fit between something I was good at doing (so I could make partner) and something I enjoyed doing (so I could go home content at night)."[33] He found that good fit as a business transactional lawyer, first drafting commercial contracts and, after

---

Facing page: James A. Baker, III. Photo provided by Baker Botts, L.L.P.

32. Baker was initially ineligible to join Baker Botts, the firm formed by his great-grandfather, where his grandfather and father had also spent their careers, because of the firm's nepotism rule. However, Baker's performance at the University of Texas Law School had been so outstanding (he was a law review editor) and his prospects otherwise appeared to be so bright, that Baker Botts's management considered waiving the nepotism rule for him. The rule proved ironclad, however, and so Baker joined the Andrews Kurth firm. Later in his life, after he left public service in 1992, Baker finally joined Baker Botts, where he continues to work to this day.

33. Baker, *The Politics of Diplomacy* (New York: G. P. Putnam's Sons, 1995), 133.

moving up the ladder, negotiating them.

His personal strengths brought him success as he came to excel in his chosen career. In particular, attorney James Baker provided his corporate clientele with the following tools in his business lawyer toolkit:

Painstaking attention to detail and foresight. Baker acknowledges he's always been a "cross the t's and dot the i's" kind of guy. And he still recites as his mantra the "5 Ps" taught by his father: "Proper preparation prevents poor performance." As a successful transactional practitioner, Baker knew his job was to anticipate the potential issues that might rear their ugly heads in a business venture and to make sure those issues were addressed with clarity on the front end in the agreements he prepared and negotiated.

Empathy. As he explained in *The Politics of Diplomacy*, to get to the goal line of consummating the deals he handled, Baker knew he not only had to know which points were crucial and which were less essential to his client, but he also knew he had to get into the heads of the lawyer and party on the other side to understand their constraints and priorities on issues. I interviewed him on June 28, 2011, at which time he told me, "You've got to know what your red lines are and what your opponent's redlines are." To make sure empathy was in play on both sides of the table, Baker also typically provided the other side with a clear picture of what circumstances were most important to his client. Using this approach, the back-and-forth of negotiations progressed from the perspective of all participants fully understanding each other's situation, allowing for a higher likelihood of moving toward an agreement.

The one-on-one power to persuade. Deals often get made or fall apart over a single disputed issue. That being the case, one side either gets its way on that final outcome determinative issue or it doesn't, meaning one side either persuades its opponent to accept its perspective on the deal-breaking point or else everyone goes home empty-handed. Persuading a counterpart to accept one's most important term, thereby allowing the agreement to get made, is what great business lawyers do on a consistent basis. Choice of words and tone are crucial to maximizing persuasion. Mutual trust and rapport also make a big difference. And maybe the most important tool required to get things to go the client's way at crunch time is the trait James Baker learned and respected during his time in the U.S. Marine Corps: the ability to project "command presence" at the moment of truth in a transaction, when the deal either makes or breaks. This force of personality combines self-confidence (without arrogance), quiet strength (without bravado), conviction in one's position, and yes, a subtle measure of charisma, all coming together to get the dominant lawyer over the hump to drive the negotiation to his desired destination.

Pragmatism. Lawyers sometimes lose sight of the forest for the trees and end up not consummating an agreement, though a good deal was possible, because they allowed their client to throw in the towel when every single issue didn't get resolved favorably. Obviously, certain key terms are essential before an acceptable agreement can be reached. He told me, "There are red lines in every deal; and you don't cross those lines." But not all points rise to deal-breaker status. Baker understood this and later named his philosophy of what it takes to get transactions closed "principled pragmatism" (during our interview, he explained, "I don't think the two terms are mutually exclusive"), defined as doing all he could to get his clients' agreements finalized, even when they achieved only some of their objectives.

Quickly reaching the heart of a matter. When James Baker was a young lawyer at Andrews Kurth, management assigned Harry Jones as his supervisor. In his memoir, *Work Hard, Study . . . and Keep out of Politics!*, Baker called Jones "a lawyer's lawyer," and gave his mentor credit for refining his "ability to separate the wheat from the chaff or, less delicately, to cut through the BS in a written memo or a face-to-face negotiation."[34] Former Senate majority leader Howard Baker (no relation) would later acknowledge James Baker as the "master

34. Baker, *Work Hard*, 13.

of the thirty-second conversation," a fact the Houston legal and business community already knew.

Finding the best opening for moving negotiations toward the goal line. Nobody gets two chances to make a strong first impression about one's plan and motivation for making a deal. James Baker's "5 Ps" caused him to brainstorm several possible discussion starters before zeroing in on the best way to get the ball rolling toward productive negotiations, knowing that using an opening that resonated with the other side's mind-set usually jump-started the flow of momentum toward the final objective, whereas getting off to a bad start often kills a possible deal before negotiations ever get off the ground.

Good timing. Since childhood, James Baker has spent much of his recreational time hunting and fishing, activities that stress the importance of patience in waiting for the right time to pull the trigger or jerk the hook. He has used that same intuitive sense of what journalist Hedrick Smith called "jugular timing" in seizing initiatives and directing priorities during his negotiations.

Knowing when to drop one's guard. When satisfied the person on the other side of the table was trustworthy and sensitive to the pertinent circumstances in play on a deal, Baker knew when to depart from a formal arm's-length attitude, shift his internal gear, and open up with candid disclosure calculated to get his counterpart to do the same. When operating in his candor mode, Baker often saw obstacles to compromise disappear in a flash, allowing progress to proceed on a faster track toward making a final agreement.

Avoiding litigation if at all possible. Unsuccessful negotiations sometimes lead to litigation. Because of its expense, risk, and time-consuming nature, fighting a lawsuit is the prudent client's least favorite sport. Knowing this, Baker conducted his negotiations, particularly those that were most tense and had the most at stake, mindful of the threat of litigation's looming presence. He always believed that the business lawyer owes his client the duty to explore all viable possibilities to save or even walk away from a deal before advocating litigation as a justifiable option.

————

Entering the year 1970, thirty-nine-year-old James Baker had (1) honed his above-described skills to a high professional level; (2) made partner and became part of management at the growing Andrews Kurth firm as his star continued to rise; (3) thrived in a strong family with his wife, Mary Stuart, and their four sons, though Mary had been battling breast cancer for over a year; and (4) developed a close friendship with his tennis doubles partner at the Houston Country Club, George H. W. Bush, who had begun to make a name for himself as the congressman representing the Gulf Coast area. But the air went out of Baker's balloon when his wife died in February 1970.

After months of grieving following his wife's death, James Baker began inflating a new balloon by jumping into a new fishbowl when he ran George Bush's 1970 campaign for the U.S. Senate in Harris County. Bush lost the race to Lloyd Bentsen, but the election caused the political bug to attach itself onto James Baker's soul, and it never let go. Though his grandfather had counseled Baker as a young man to "work hard, study . . . and keep out of politics," the forty-year-old widower decided he would call his own shots in facing this crossroads in his life: "Participating in George's campaign for the Senate had awakened a sense of adventure and high challenge that was missing from the daily practice of law. I wasn't ready to quit the practice or run for office, but I was ready for something different."[35]

Baker's next foray into politics came two years later in running President Nixon's reelection campaign in the Houston area, even though he later (like so many millions of Americans) came to deplore the president's malfeasance in the Watergate incident. Soon after Nixon's reelection in November 1972, the country became obsessed with the investigation and prosecution of Watergate misconduct, and that national distraction lasted two years, until Nixon resigned from the presidency and a month later was pardoned by President

35. Ibid., 22.

Gerald Ford. All the political and legal drama from Watergate temporarily stalled James Baker's momentum for public service, though it gave him time in 1973 to marry Susan Garrett Winston and meld her and her three children with his own brood.

At George Bush's suggestion, in 1975, President Ford's secretary of commerce, Rogers Morton, asked Baker to become his right hand man/undersecretary. Baker accepted, moved his family to Washington, DC, and soon endeared himself not only to Morton but also to President Ford and his chief of staff, Dick Cheney, with his smarts, "can do" attitude, and work ethic. Ford and Cheney saw quickly what James Baker's corporate clientele and law firm partners in Houston already knew—that he had a rare dual capacity for not only seeing what needed to be done but actually getting things done.

Facing a closely contested race for president in the 1976 Republican primaries against California governor Ronald Reagan, Gerald Ford chose Baker, his favorite "new kid on the block," for the key campaign position of maintaining the commitments of his elected delegates and persuading undecided delegates to support him. Baker's one-on-one power to persuade proved instrumental in Ford's eking out a victory over Reagan by only 117 delegates (out of 2,257) at the Republican National Convention in Kansas City. Witnessing the "new kid's" astonishing performance throughout Ford's campaign and assistance in securing Ford's nomination by the Republican Party, the *New York Times* nicknamed Baker "Miracle Man."

When the Republican Convention ended, President Ford promoted his chief delegate hunter to serve as the chairman of his entire campaign committee. Pundits expressed shock over Ford's giving an apparent novice such a massive responsibility, particularly in the context of pre-convention polls that showed Ford trailing Democratic nominee Jimmy Carter by 33 percent. As the country would soon learn, James Baker was no ordinary political rookie.

President Ford got a bounce coming out of the Kansas City convention and only trailed Carter by 12 percent. The bounce soon faded, however, and Carter's lead grew to 18 percent by mid-September before the first presidential debate. Ford's chances for keeping his job appeared hopeless, but by mid-October, Baker's campaign leadership was instrumental to his candidate narrowing the gap to only 1 percent. Then Gerald Ford proceeded not only to shoot himself in the foot but to blow both his legs off, getting confused in the second presidential debate and claiming that "there is no Soviet domination of Eastern Europe." Baker's damage-control efforts almost succeeded in putting Humpty Dumpty back together again, but Ford ultimately lost to Carter in an electoral college squeaker: 297 to 240, the closest presidential election since 1916.

After serving in the Ford administration, attending meetings in the Oval Office, being a guest on *Face the Nation*, and quarterbacking a national presidential campaign, forty-six-year-old James Baker left Washington, DC, in 1976 and headed back to his law office at Andrews Kurth, knowing that the business of billing time while advising corporate clients had lost its luster, particularly after seeing how valuable his legal skills as counselor, negotiator, deal maker, and advocate had proven to be in the national political arena.

Returning to Houston from Washington, James Baker didn't sit in his law office long before deciding he wanted to run for political office. George Bush encouraged his friend to enter the Texas governor's race in 1978, but Baker rejected the advice and ran as the Republican nominee for attorney general of Texas, thinking that position would be a better fit for him. The job may have been a better fit, but at a time when the Republican Party in Texas was still in its embryonic stage, Baker received only 44.4 percent of the vote and lost to moderate Democrat Mark White.

James Baker had barely caught his breath following his hectic campaign for attorney general when George Bush called, confirmed his long-held desire to run for president, and got his former doubles partner to agree to serve as his national campaign director. Immediately, fundraising and assembling a national organization consumed Baker's life, and by January 1980, he took a leave of absence from Andrews Kurth and moved back to Washington.

With Baker flicking the levers, Bush exceeded expectations and started off 1980 winning both the Maine straw poll and the Iowa caucus; but when Ronald Reagan won the New Hampshire primary, the California governor gained a lead he never lost and became the Republican presidential nominee at the Detroit convention in 1980, selecting George Bush as his running mate.

Until then, James Baker had worked for candidates (Ford and Bush) who had opposed Ronald Reagan. Despite that, the new Republican nominee asked Baker to negotiate the details of his upcoming presidential debates, a task perfectly suited to the lawyer who had mastered his craft as a hard trader in the business trenches of Houston. Democratic counterpart Jody Powell later described the exercise of negotiating the debate agreement with Baker as a process of "bluff and counterbluff, scheming, conniving, and hard-nosed horse trading."[36] In *Work Hard*, the Republican negotiator described how he agreed to Carter's being permitted to stand on a riser during the debate to appear to have equal height to Reagan, but Baker got "something good in return" (unspecified) for making that concession.

Besides asking his former adversary to get the debate deal struck on favorable terms, Reagan also gave Baker the responsibility for his debate preparation. In performing this task, the one-time Houston litigator staged mock trials for his newly adopted Republican candidate. Amazingly, Jimmy Carter chose to boycott the first presidential debate because the League of Women Voters (as sponsors) had invited third-party candidate John Anderson to participate, and Carter only wanted to debate Reagan. The debate still took place as scheduled on September 21, 1980, pitting Anderson against Reagan. To prepare for the nationally televised war of words with Anderson, in a perfectly staged mock trial at the Virginia country estate of Senator John Warner (and his then wife Elizabeth Taylor), Baker selected David Stockman (who later became President Reagan's budget director) to play the role of Anderson; John Tower, Alan Greenspan, Jeane Kirkpatrick, and Howard Baker to play the part of media questioners; and Bill Casey, Ed Meese, Mike Deaver, David Gergen, TV consultant Bill Carruthers, and Frank Hodsoll (Baker's Commerce Department aide) to watch and critique Reagan's performance.

For the first time, during the rigorous debate rehearsals (which lasted for hours, involved a barrage of tough questions, and were

---

36. Ibid., 111–112.

videotaped to allow the candidate to critique his own performance), Ronald and Nancy Reagan got to see, up close and personal, James Baker's attention to detail, powers of anticipation, and commanding presence in live, real time. Both liked what they saw.

After the properly prepared Reagan's stellar performance in the first debate, during which he manhandled Anderson, Anderson's voting support disappeared to the extent that the second and final debate held October 28 in Cleveland included only Carter and Reagan. Again, Baker masterfully prepared his candidate with mock trials, and again a very confident Reagan performed with megawatt star power and blew away Carter with the killer lines, "There you go again," and "Are you better off than you were four years ago?"

Less than a week after the Cleveland debate, Ronald Reagan annihilated incumbent president Jimmy Carter, winning the electoral votes of forty-four states, making his margin of victory 489-44. When it came time after election night to pick the adviser to serve in the coveted position of White House chief of staff in his new administration, Reagan surprised everyone by choosing his debate coach—who in five years had transformed himself from a Houston business transactional lawyer into a national political titan.

THE REAGAN YEARS

From January 1981 to August 1988, James Baker served President Reagan for four years as his White House chief of staff and almost four years as his secretary of the treasury. In those roles, he was the ultimate Washington insider, excelling in what Pulitzer Prize–winning journalist Hedrick Smith called "the power game." Mr. Smith became so intrigued by DC's favorite sport, particularly in how it was played in the 1980s, that he authored a 726-page best-selling book about it, appropriately titled *The Power Game.*

Arriving at the nation's capital as a writer for the *New York Times* in 1962, for twenty-six years Hedrick Smith had encountered hundreds (if not thousands) of politicians and bureaucrats who worked inside federal government by the time he wrote *The Power Game.* Out of all those whose performance he observed, Smith recognized James Baker as a grand master. To clarify his subject, Smith defined exactly what the "power game" was in his book's introduction:

> The games politicians play today—that is, how the power games are played and therefore how Washington *really* works—have unwritten rules, rituals, and patterns that explain why things so often happen the way they do. . . .
>
> Washington is a city engaged simultaneously in substance and in stratagems. Principles become intertwined with power plays. For Washington is as much moved by who's up and who's down, who's in and who's out, as it is by setting policy. . . .
>
> In the special world of Washington, [politicians] hotly pursue their highly personal interests in the inside power games—turf games, access games, career games, money games, blame games—each of which has an inner logic of its own. . . .
>
> The real pros, like chess masters, rarely trust true amateurism in politics. They usually have a pretty good feel for how certain policy lines and maneuvers will play out, before they start. . . .
>
> In all of this, power is the mysterious quotient. Power is the ability to make something happen or to keep it from happening. It can spring from tactical ingenuity and jugular timing, or simply from knowing more than anyone else at the critical moment of decision.[37]

Ronald Reagan's every move during his first term as president was guided by three men—counselor to the president Edwin Meese, deputy chief of staff Michael Deaver, and chief of staff James Baker. Pundits early on dubbed them "the troika." Though Meese and Deaver had worked closely with Reagan for years in California, and Baker was a newcomer in the president's world, it soon became clear to Hedrick Smith and everyone else that James Baker had the dominant influence among the troika because of his interpersonal and strategic skills.

In his book, Smith analyzed how Baker understood and executed on "the five keys to power in the White House" to become

---

37. Smith, *The Power Game* (New York: Ballantine Books, 1988), xv–xvii, xxi–xxii.

President Reagan's most trusted adviser, instrumental in guiding the nation's chief executive to his greatest achievements during his highly successful first term. Those five keys were the following:

- Division of duties: establish clearly defined roles and make sure to have the last crack at everything going to and from the president.

Using the 5 Ps that had brought him success in his prior jobs as a lawyer and campaign organizer, Baker grasped the import of Alexander Haig's "three main levels of power"—managing the flow of paper, the president's schedule, and the press—which served to confirm the advice Baker had received from Dick Cheney and had served both Haig and Cheney well in maximizing their roles when they had held the chief of staff position for Presidents Nixon and Ford. Daily meetings of the troika were held in Baker's corner office in the West Wing, with the host sitting at the head of the table and Meese and Deaver agreeing that everything should go through that one office before being presented to the president.

- Forge an alliance with someone trusted by the president: when participating in a three-person management team, be in the majority.

Baker's street smarts, positive personality, command presence, and empathy attracted Michael Deaver into his magnetic fold, which proved not only crucial to Baker's achieving the dominant position in the troika but also enhanced his status with Nancy Reagan. Besides the president, the first lady's other best friend was Michael Deaver. So when Deaver fully embraced Baker as his West Wing comrade in arms, that tight relationship spoke volumes to Mrs. Reagan. In his book *President Reagan: The Role of a Lifetime*, veteran *Washington Post* White House correspondent Lou Cannon explained exactly what Baker did to cultivate his important relationship with Deaver to make sure he always had the control position in the troika:

> Baker, however, recognized that Deaver had a cool analytical side and had applied it to understanding the Reagans.

He turned over the schedule to Deaver and depended
upon him for daily assessments of the mood, capacities,
and preferences of the first family. He relied almost totally upon Deaver's advice before embarking on any venture
that required participation of the president.[38]

• Have a strong support team: assemble the most talented and
  loyal staff possible.

James Baker knew from his years at Andrews Kurth that having
the best brains on one's side usually translates into getting the best
work product and the best final results. He maintained that top talent standard for his personal support team during his years as chief
of staff. In particular, he chose Richard Darman (who had worked
for Baker at the Commerce Department) to serve under him in the
position of President Reagan's staff secretary. Darman was not only
in charge of the paper flow that landed on the president's desk but
also became the chief of staff's right-hand person in taking on full
responsibility for mastering the most complex policy issues. Baker
recognized that Darman matched up in pure intellectual horsepower with the top students at Princeton that Baker had known in his
college days, the law school whiz kids with whom he had worked
as an editor of the *Texas Law Review*, and the brightest lawyers in
Houston, so he plugged in Darman's high-octane smarts where his
services could be most strategically used. He also hired Margaret
Tutwiler to serve as his assistant, who, according to Lou Cannon in
The Role, "served as Baker's eyes and ears among the White House
press corps, where she was valued for integrity and frank appraisals
that spared not even Baker."[39]

• Create a vast support network outside the White House: through
  goodwill, build easy-access bridges into Congress and the media.

With almost no exceptions, throughout his life, whenever James
Baker has decided he wants to have a long-term, positive personal

---

38. Cannon, *President Reagan: The Role of a Lifetime* (New York: PublicAffairs, 1991), 88.
39. Ibid., 494.

relationship with someone else, then the odds of a friendship getting formed on a fast track are exponentially high. Hedrick Smith provided this telling description of what one encountered in Baker's immediate presence during the Reagan years:

> Tall, trim, thin-lipped, handsome, always impeccably dressed and shined, and cool as a Texas gunslinger . . . Baker is smart, cautious, patient, and decisive. He is savvy; he sees the interrelationships of issues, people, money, and votes, and he marshals his own forces extremely well. As I interviewed Baker or watched him in action, the one word that kept coming to mind was *control*: self-control, control of the situation, control of others. Baker keeps his intentions to himself or shares them with only a couple of trusted aides; he plots his moves with care, and strikes when confident of a kill. He stalks his political prey with his pale-blue eyes set in a squint, gauging the political terrain and counting votes the way he would watch the skies or listen for the telltale rustle of a gobbler. He thrives on challenge. And he exults in the sport of politics and, most of all, in winning.[40]

Who in Congress, the media, or anywhere else wouldn't want to have a close friendship with someone who measures up to that description?

In *The Role*, Lou Cannon gave the specifics of exactly what Baker did to bond with Congress and the media:

> James Baker worked sixteen-hour days courting Congress and cultivating the media. He never left his White House office without returning every phone call that had been made to him that day by a member of Congress, however obscure. He devoted several hours of every week explaining the administration's goals, motives, strategy, and tactics to White House reporters for the networks, news magazines, wire services, and major newspapers, advanc-

---

40. Smith, *The Power Game*, 313.

ing himself with this accessibility but advancing Reagan
even more. Baker was truthful with reporters, which won
them over, and he held their interest by discreetly sharing
his political insights with selected members of the White
House press corps. His political experience had taught
him to trust reporters, up to a point, and the value of
establishing a working relationship with them in advance
of crises.[41]

• Be action and results oriented: spend one's time as a player on
  the field, not as a spectator in the grandstands.

In his preface to *The Politics of Diplomacy*, James Baker acknowledged that he has always considered himself more a person of action
than reflection and later in the book said that "my study of the law
probably reinforced my emphasis on action over contemplation."[42]
Hedrick Smith put this reality of Baker's persona into words in
The Power Game:

> Baker understood that in the chaotic, hothouse world of
> Washington, there was no such thing as separating strat-
> egy from tactics, long-term policy planning from short-
> term actions, policy from politics. He knew they had to
> be integrated and that often tactics can drive strategy and
> the immediate can overcome the long-term.[43]

A key to success in any job is to do one's best to make the boss
look good. Chief of Staff James Baker used that time-tested principle to help Ronald Reagan's first term be filled with achievements.
Reagan pushed through the legislation he wanted because of his
great relationship with Congress, which came in large part through
James Baker's great relationship with Congress. Furthermore,
Reagan for the most part avoided costly mistakes because his chief
of staff could spot potential problems on the horizon. In Baker's
words, as chief of staff, he "caught the javelins" before they skew-

---

41. Cannon, *The Role*, 90.

42. Baker, *The Politics of Diplomacy*, 40.

43. Smith, *The Power Game*, 319.

ered the president.

Above all, what allowed James Baker to succeed as chief of staff (and in all his government positions) was adhering to his "cardinal rule," which he described when I interviewed him: "I had a cardinal rule. And I told my presidents this. It's not what you do in Washington that gets you in trouble; it's when you don't tell the truth and try to cover up—that's where people get in trouble."

———————

As the chief of staff and the president quickly developed strong positive chemistry, Baker began acting exactly as he would have had he been Reagan's personal attorney/counselor, using the same tools that had served the lawyer so well with his clients in Houston. During our interview, he explained why he saw no distinction between the way he counseled clients as a lawyer and the way he counseled presidents and other dignitaries:

> I think certain things are true with respect to both. You've got to be as candid and honest with your client as you are with the president of the United States. Many clients don't want to hear what you have to tell them. Same thing is true of presidents. You have to have the strength of your convictions, and tell him what you think, knowing he may not follow your advice, because he has the final say. After all, he's the guy who got elected.

Painstaking attention to detail and foresight. Knowing of Ed Meese's disappointment in being passed over for chief of staff by Reagan (though Meese did receive the cabinet rank position of counselor to the president for policy with an office in the West Wing) and seeing in advance the high likelihood that their respective positions could easily overlap in performing their duties (and thereby cause them to come into conflict), in mid-November 1988 (i.e., two months before starting to work in the White House), Baker prepared a memo that specifically identified the responsibilities of each man in his job. He then allowed Meese to review and tweak the memo, and finally they both initialed it, officially signing off on it. This meeting of the minds proved instrumental in their avoiding turf battles for the next four years.

If ever a president of the United States needed a chief of staff who took on every responsibility from a hard-nosed 5-Ps perspective, it was Ronald Reagan. In *The Role*, Lou Cannon recounts how on the night in 1983 before President Reagan was scheduled to preside over an international economic summit at Williamsburg, Virginia, Baker brought his boss a thick briefing book so he would be prepared. When the chief of staff arrived the next morning to accompany the president to the summit, the briefing book lay on the table exactly where Baker had left it the night before. Reagan explained that he had not gotten around to opening the book, because "Well, Jim, *The Sound of Music* was on last night."[44]

Empathy. In *Work Hard*, Baker expressed how his empathetic powers as a lawyer translated into politics in general and into the Reagan White House in particular:

> The best way to persuade someone to see things your way is to start by trying to see things his way. You need to understand and respect the political imperatives that guide his action, then to deal with both the person and his politics in a civil and respectful way. I learned as a corporate lawyer that, more often than not, negotiators who worked in this way could find a common path that served the needs of both sides. President Reagan was a master at doing this; he told me he had cut his teeth as a negotiator when he was president of the Screen Actors Guild.[45]

The one-on-one power to persuade + quickly reaching the heart of a matter + knowing when to drop one's guard. In 1983, concerned about media leaks that appeared to have come from inside the White House, national security adviser William Clark (with the support of Ed Meese but without James Baker's knowledge or approval) got President Reagan to sign off on a memo authorizing the

---

44. Cannon, *The Role*, 36.
45. Baker, *Work Hard*, 155.

FBI to conduct lie detector examinations on all those having access to confidential information. When Baker learned of the memo, he became so outraged at the prospect of having Vice President Bush, Secretary of State Schultz, the troika, and other top presidential advisers strapped down and wired up on the polygraph table that he burst into an Oval Office meeting President Reagan was holding at the time with Bush and Schultz. In no uncertain terms, he expressed his strong feelings about the memo, explaining that the media would have a field day telling the public about the extreme level of mistrust inside the Reagan administration as evidenced by their all being required to submit to lie detectors. Reagan heard his chief of staff, reflected on the heated and potent advice, and immediately revoked the memo, as Baker proved his one-on-one power to persuade the president at a moment of truth in their relationship.

Pragmatism. It didn't take Baker long to realize that he and Ronald Reagan shared a philosophy of "principled pragmatism" in getting deals done. Baker explained this in *Work Hard*:

> [President Reagan] was much more a pragmatist than an ideologue. Yes, he had strong convictions and principles, but he was willing to compromise to get the best deal he could. "Jim," he would often tell me as we discussed strategy, "I'd rather get eighty percent of what I want than to go over the cliff with my flag flying."
>
> By contrast, many of his less pragmatic followers hated compromise. To them, it was better to lose everything than to give an inch. They didn't understand how the system works. Pragmatism without principles is cynicism, but principle without pragmatism is often powerless. To turn ideas into policies, a leader must be prepared to fight hard—yes—but also to accept victory on the terms that can be won, even when they are short of perfection. That's the reality of politics. My leader called me to his service because he wanted to change things, not die trying, and he thought I could help.[46]

---

46. Ibid., 125.

Finding the best opening for gaining momentum to get to the goal line. One of President Reagan's greatest achievements during his first term was getting tax reform and cuts enacted in two segments during his first year in office. His tax reform empowered the economic recovery from the Carter administration's dark days when the "misery index" of high inflation plus high unemployment exceeded 20 percent. Initially, the Democratic-controlled House opposed the legislation. How to turn enough Democrats around to get the first tax bill passed? Use the right opening! Baker decided that the best way to win the battle in the House was to use his best shot first and expect that opening to create momentum toward passage of the bill. He soon determined that the best shot for getting the scales to tip was plugging the "Great Communicator" directly into both the congressional and the public psyche, using Ronald Reagan live and in person—in his speeches to and breakfasts with Congress and in televised speeches to the public.

Using this strategy to open strong, there was President Reagan, front and center to his audience in April 1981, fresh from a blowout November election victory that definitely gave him a political mandate, and also heroically recovered (at age seventy) from an assassin's bullet that had hospitalized him one month before. When the new president spoke to Congress for the first time with his message "Let us work together," applause interrupted the speech sixteen times. When he went back the second time on April 28 and told the legislators that the American people had waited long enough and wanted action, it was all over but the crying for the liberal Democrats who refused to support his tax plan. Speaker of the House Tip O'Neill stated the obvious: "I can read Congress. They go with the will of the people, and the will of the people is to go along with the president."[47] Reaganomics tax reform passed the House 253-176 on May 7.

Good timing. President Reagan realized that he couldn't get all the tax relief from Congress that he favored for the American people at once. Taking too big a bite always produces an upset stomach. Instead, the Reagan administration's plan for tax relief came in two

---

47. Ibid., 179.

carefully timed stages, allowing congressional leaders to digest the tax cuts at an acceptable pace. Reagan's second major tax bill, with cuts that exceeded the first, passed the House on July 27 and was signed into law August 13, 1981.

Aversion to interpersonal warfare. In 1984, James Baker and Michael Deaver came up with a personnel change idea that they believed would be beneficial to the Reagan administration—shifting Baker over to become the president's national security adviser (a position most recently held by Bill Clark, but who had just been named as the new secretary of the interior, following James Watt's resignation) and then moving Deaver up to chief of staff. Baker explained the reasoning behind the proposed job change: "Deaver and I were trying to get all the operations of the White House under one roof. Until then, we didn't have control of the foreign policy side. We thought our plan would allow for better coordination within the Reagan administration."[48]

In following the "5 Ps" mandate of "proper preparation," before discussing the job change idea with the president, Baker and Deaver ran it by Vice President Bush; Secretary of State Schultz; Reagan's California campaign manager, Stu Spencer; and the first lady, all of whom backed it. With that level of support, Baker and Deaver then took their idea to the president, who initially approved it. However, when Reagan told Bill Clark who his successor would be, Clark opposed the move vigorously (as Baker had definitely become his White House nemesis in the aftermath of their confrontation over the lie detector) and quickly lined up the counselor to the president, Ed Meese; CIA director Bill Casey; Secretary of Defense Weinberger; and American ambassador to the UN, Jeane Kilpatrick to support him. Battle lines were drawn. When Baker learned of the looming conflict among Reagan's top insiders, he went to the Oval Office and said, "Mr. President, I don't want to be a problem for you. If there's that much opposition, let's forget it."[49] Reagan followed Baker's war-

---

48. James Baker, personal communication to author, June 28, 2011.
49. Baker, *Work Hard*, 201.

averse counsel, avoided an interpersonal war, and lived to regret it.[50]

Following President Reagan's reelection in November 1984, a thoroughly exhausted James Baker left the all-consuming position of chief of staff (after holding the job for the third longest time in American history) to accept an offer by Donald Regan, President Reagan's first-term secretary of the treasury, to switch jobs for Reagan's second term. The change of chiefs of staff transformed the Reagan presidency from Baker's reasonably smooth sailing on consistently calm waters to Regan's barely keeping the boat afloat in traversing constantly choppy seas. In *The Role*, Lou Cannon explained how James Baker and Donald Regan performed the same job for the same president and achieved very different results:

> Because of Reagan's passivity, his presidency easily assumed the coloration of whoever was running the White House. Baker's and Regan's styles were totally contrasting. Where Baker was collegial, Regan was directive. Where Baker was cautious, Regan was bold. Baker preferred to operate behind the scenes, forging a political consensus and framing it in terms that Reagan could endorse. Regan charged ahead, dismissing arguments he disagreed with as readily as he had dismissed contrary opinions at Merrill Lynch. He liked the limelight and repeatedly drew attention to his personal role. (Baker and Deaver were horrified when Regan instructed that he be introduced as "White House chief of staff" at the president's out-of-town appearances.) Baker and Deaver had been protective of Reagan to a fault, always sensitive to the possibility of self-inflicted wounds. Regan was unmindful of the president's blind spots and exposed him to damaging

---

50. Reagan later acknowledged that he made a serious error by not making the job change Baker and Deaver wanted. Baker explained why in *Work Hard*:

> Seven years later, former President Reagan reflected in his autobiography on the impact of that hassle: "My decision not to appoint Jim Baker as national security adviser, I suppose, was a turning point for my administration, although I had no idea at the time how significant it would prove to be."
>
> How so? One hyphenated word: Iran-Contra. The president was suggesting that if I had been his national security adviser—rather than Bud McFarlane and Bud's successor, John Poindexter, a retired admiral—the scandal that rocked the administration during its second term might never have happened. (202)

controversies on Bitburg and South Africa that a more prudent chief of staff would have avoided.[51]

As head of the Treasury Department from February 1985 until August 1988, James Baker used his same lawyer toolkit; his same talented White House staff of Dick Darman, Margaret Tutwiler, and John Rogers; and his continued implementation of Hedrick Smith's five keys to White House power, and he took all of them to his new cabinet position. There, for his most significant achievement, he obtained passage of the Tax Reform Act of 1986, which essentially reduced taxes for individuals at the expense of raising taxes for businesses (by closing loopholes). Baker's playing the power game against both the executive and legislative branches of government put him into conflict first with his predecessor, Don Regan, whose own prior proposed tax bill would be nullified and superseded by Baker's proposed tax bill, and then into even more conflict with conservative House Republicans, who didn't want businesses to lose their tax breaks. The clanging discord within his own party caused President Reagan to remain neutral for a while over this important domestic policy. Finally, largely due to Baker's one-on-one persuasion, the president came around and endorsed his current secretary of the treasury's bill.

After obtaining the president's support, to get his party's legislators on track, James Baker jumped from the Treasury Department grandstands onto the playing field and personally lobbied House Republicans to get them to support his bill. He explained why in *Work Hard*:

> Was it unusual for a cabinet member to play politics like I did here, at least so publicly? The answer is yes. I rolled up my sleeves and got involved in the grunt work because of the importance of the issue, because of what it meant politically to the president, and because I knew how to do it. I had spent four years as chief of staff shepherding legislation through Congress on behalf of Ronald

---

51. Cannon, *The Role*, 498.

Reagan. And let's face it: I also knew that if we lost, my reputation and effectiveness would have taken a big hit.[52]

Exactly what did Secretary of the Treasury Baker (accompanied by top lieutenant Richard Darman) say in his arm-twisting conversations with House swing voters that got them to support his bill? Hedrick Smith answered the question in *The Power Game*:

> Baker and Darman used one well-tested power-game ploy to lure back some rebels: Lott and Cheney wanted no compromise, but Michel, like other Republicans, was stunned to see Reagan humiliated [over the bill's initially being voted down from even reaching the House floor], and wanted to help him. So did Kemp, who needed tax reform kept alive as the banner for his presidential bid. But Kemp and Michel required some fig leaf to justify Republicans' switching back to Reagan's side. The ploy used by Baker and Darman had worked well on other tough votes, such as the AWACS sale to Saudi Arabia in 1981 and various *contra*-aid votes. With Kemp, they crafted a letter containing pledges from Reagan to placate House Republicans. If they would let Rostenkowski's plan pass, Reagan pledged to pressure the Senate for a better version. He promised to veto any bill with an individual tax rate over thirty-five percent and lacking a $2,000 personal exemption (a Kemp proviso), and he made some nice-sounding but spongy promises about protecting incentives for capital-intensive industries. In congressional lingo, that provided "cover" for vote switchers.
>
> But the key to reviving the tax-reform coalition was to change the issue—from the contents of the tax bill to saving the president. Not only was Reagan immensely popular with Republicans, but they were counting on him to help them in the 1986 elections. It was stupid for them

---

52. Baker, *Work Hard*, 231.

to mortally wound him now, and the White House played that theme hard.[53]

Finally, as he almost always did, Baker prevailed in this most hotly contested round of the power game, and got both Houses of Congress to pass the bill on September 27, allowing President Reagan to sign into law the Tax Reform Act of 1986 on October 22, 1986. With this astounding political victory, James Baker proved once and for all time to Hedrick Smith and everyone else that no one, absolutely no one, could make things work and win the day in our nation's capital like the business lawyer from Houston. President Reagan expressed it best in his letter accepting Baker's resignation in August 1988 (allowing Baker to focus on George Bush's presidential campaign): "In your career you have set an important example. You have clearly demonstrated that the best of the political arts can be combined with first-class professionalism in the effective pursuit of America's interests."[54]

When George H. W. Bush got elected as the forty-first president of the United States in November 1988, he made his first major decision shortly after his acceptance speech. President-elect Bush determined that in his new job, he would need by his side the shrewdest person he knew to serve as his secretary of state, since that chosen person would be charged with the seemingly impossible task of keeping the highly volatile world under some measure of control. The chosen person, of course, was James Baker.

THE BUSH YEARS

In the book on his term as president that he co-authored with his national security adviser, Brent Scowcroft, *A World Transformed* (New York: Alfred A. Knopf, 1998), George Bush explained that he selected James Baker as his secretary of state because he and Baker had been friends for many years, had collaborated during Bush's second run for the Senate, and because he considered Baker to be a real fighter, a strong negotiator, and someone who would honestly and forcefully give his opinions on matters.

---

53. Smith, *The Power Game*, 503.

54. Baker, *Work Hard*, 242.

For his own book *The Politics of Diplomacy*, which he described as his "personal narrative" of his years as secretary of state, James Baker chose the subtitle: *Revolution, War & Peace, 1989–1992*. Having graduated from his Houston legal and business battles, to running national presidential campaigns, to catching javelins in the White House, to succeeding in the halls of Congress, Baker had proved to himself and everyone else that with his skills as a counselor, nego-tiator, and deal maker, he could play college ball without breaking a sweat and could absolutely dominate minor league competition; but at last the time had come when he would get to prove his ultimate mettle, in the big leagues of international hardball, where one's in-box is often filled with communications addressing revolution, war, and peace from around the world.

Just as elite athletes see the pace of their games accelerate with each step up the competition ladder, so it was for James Baker in moving from lawyer to national statesman to international diplomat. Baker expressed to me in a personal interview the following:

> In politics, the time frame is so compressed. You are mak-ing decisions very much in real time. When I was practic-ing law, looking back on it now, I think I had more time to consider what my moves should be than I had in poli-tics, where decisions had to be made in days, sometimes hours, and sometimes minutes; and there are huge penal-ties for being wrong, because unlike a business negotia-tion, political negotiations are often a zero sum game.

Another major challenge in political diplomacy as opposed to mere lawyering in private practice is the number of players from different teams who are all engaging with each other simultaneously. Baker elaborated on this during our interview:

> When you're negotiating in a law practice, everything's pinpointed against the guy across the table. When you're in public service as secretary of the treasury or secretary of state or White House chief of staff, you're dealing with many different constituencies. You've got to address congressional considerations, press considerations, the

public interest considerations, other foreign countries' considerations, and many others.

With the higher speed in making tougher decisions in a zero-sum game, coupled with more factions with whom to contend simultaneously, Baker (a rugby player at Princeton) has often said, "Politics ain't beanbag. It's a bloodsport." During our interview, Baker told me, "being secretary of state was the best job I ever had. You're playing in the biggest of the big leagues. You're negotiating for your country. It's like competing for your country in the Olympics."

Having had his way in the power games of Washington, DC, for eight consecutive years during the Reagan presidency, Baker had confidence in his grasp of politics and diplomacy. But what exactly were the "politics" and "diplomacy" that he had mastered? Here's how Baker explained the two words in the preface to *The Politics of Diplomacy*:

> Politics (in its larger sense—as opposed to specific electoral campaigns) and policy are inextricably linked. It's only through politics that we can transform philosophy into policy. This is particularly true in geopolitics, where the difference between success and failure is often measured by the ability (or lack thereof) to understand how political constraints inevitably shape the outcome of any negotiation. Indeed, I would argue, with a nod to Clausewitz, that diplomacy *is* the continuation of politics—whether in revolution, war, or peace. . . .
>
> The political skill extends beyond one-on-one relations to the task of building coalitions. . . . To be successful over time, the politician-diplomat also needs to win the confidence of others. That means words must be matched by deeds and promises must be kept. . . .
>
> An American political diplomat should always remember that power divorced from the purposes valued by our democracy will ultimately prove empty. . . .

> I trust and believe that my political experience made me
> a more effective advocate, negotiator, and diplomat,
> which is why I call this book *The Politics of Diplomacy*.[55]

As demonstrated earlier in this chapter, James Baker's successful legal experience provided him with the foundation for his successful political experience. In turn, as demonstrated in the rest of this chapter, his legal and political experience combined to provide him with the foundation for his successful diplomatic experience, as they all connected in a continuum.

His 672-page book *The Politics of Diplomacy* provided his day-to-day (and sometimes moment-to-moment) international "war stories," allowing the public to grasp how he acted as secretary of state in the Bush administration by applying his legal and political skills toward diplomatic initiatives and achievements. In *Work Hard*, James Baker described the import of his book *The Politics of Diplomacy*:

> It testifies to the vindication of American leadership un-
> der both Democrats and Republicans, beginning after
> World War II with Dean Acheson's generation and cli-
> maxing four decades later with mine. It tells how to effec-
> tively organize the foreign and security policy apparatus
> of the United States government. And of the liberation
> of hundreds of millions of men, women, and children
> in Eastern Europe and Central Asia; of the triumph of
> democracy, free markets, and the rule of law; of the dra-
> matic and peaceful end of the superpower nuclear threat;
> and of freedom for Kuwait and new hopes for peace in
> the Middle East. And at a personal level, *The Politics of
> Diplomacy* is also one man's testimony to the privilege of
> having served as our nation's secretary of state in a time
> of war, revolution, and peace.[56]

Baker's specific talents honed during his Houston years as a business lawyer, as further developed by him in national politics during

---

55. Baker, *The Politics of Diplomacy*, xiv–xvi.

56. Baker, *Work Hard*, 346.

the Reagan years, continued to work well for him as he amplified them as secretary of state in the Bush years.

Painstaking attention to detail and foresight. How can anyone in a fast-moving, constantly changing, and seemingly unpredictable world possess long-term foresight? Baker explained in *The Politics of Diplomacy* how he developed his powers of anticipation as secretary of state by attending to the specific details that made up the big picture:

> In my thinking, I approached the world of 1989 from the "inside out," much the way I had approached politics and government. I started with an overall notion of where we wanted to go, and worked backward from that goal, beginning with those institutions that we had to control or influence the most in order to achieve our objective: first, the immediate bureaucracy; second, the Congress; and third, the press. Once we had done what we could in this regard, we would work on ensuring our "continental base" (relations with Canada, Mexico, and Central America), then strengthening and, where necessary, expanding our alliances across the Atlantic and Pacific.[57]

Having foresight on both small details and the big picture is obviously a valuable tool for an international diplomat, but beyond the "vision thing," he must also have the wherewithal to connect the dots that lead to the ultimate achievement of his long-term goals. From his first day on the job as secretary of state, like all his predecessors, for one of his long-term goals, James Baker aspired to achieve an acceptable level of stability in the Middle East. To move toward that objective, he had to inspire the leaders of that region to think differently and specifically about how to proceed on a going-forward basis in dealing with their neighbors. Essentially, Baker had to get them to read, comprehend, and buy into his detailed script for diplomatic progress, and the script he provided them had to contain more than vague generalities. For example, here was the script overview James Baker gave Israeli prime minister Yitzhak Shamir in his

---

57. Baker, *The Politics of Diplomacy*, 42.

letter of March 24, 1989:

> I wrote Shamir on March 24 at the President's request,
> saying that he and the Palestinians must find a way to talk
> to one another. "The people of Israel have told you to
> be cautious and tough, and those are sound pieces of ad-
> vice," I added. "But I think they have also sent a mes-
> sage to your neighbors that peace is possible—provided
> the Palestinians demonstrate they are responsible part-
> ners. This is the measure of commitment which you, as
> a statesman, can determine through diplomacy. And it is
> something that the United States and Israel, as strategic
> partners, can achieve."[58]

Empathy as the best opening for starting negotiations. After
sending the March 24, 1989, letter to Shamir, James Baker knew he
needed to have a face-to-face meeting with him, to go from overview
to specifics, and that meeting occurred two weeks later on April 5,
1989. The secretary of state's opening statement not only demonstrated his empathy for Shamir but also subtly challenged him to get
on the same page with Baker's script. From *The Politics of Diplomacy*:

> "Mr. Prime Minister," I said, "we both know that the
> media like to pigeonhole people with catchphrases.
> You've been described to me as a man of principle who
> is incapable of being practical. I've probably been de-
> scribed to you as a man totally lacking in principle who
> cares *only* about being practical. Let me tell you, like
> you, I'm very much a man who believes in principle,
> but I also think you have to be practical if you're go-
> ing to realize your principles. I also suspect you're more
> practical than your reputation. I think that you and
> I may be able to surprise some people by working
> together."[59]

---

58. Ibid., 119.
59. Ibid.

How could anyone respond negatively to such a (properly prepared) warm-hearted, self-deprecating, honest opening?

The one-on-one power to persuade. The power to persuade sometimes comes down to finding the right word on which all parties can agree. In attempting to get congressional endorsement for President Bush's policy toward Central America, thereby allowing the secretary of state's words to have genuine credibility when Baker expressed the federal government's position in his communications with our neighbors to the south, Baker ran into conflict with some Democratic senators (most notably Chris Dodd) over exactly how to state our policy toward the contras. The Democrats wanted the policy statement to say that the United States would only provide aid for "relocation" of the contras. Republicans believed using the word *relocation* would send a message that our policy, in fact, was to disband the contras. Baker, in attempting to find words for the policy that could be acceptable to both parties, initially favored the word *reintegration* over *relocation*, but that didn't quite suit them. So he worked with leaders of both parties, persuading them, as a mediator, to accept the happy-medium verbiage everyone could live with: to wit, the United States' policy in Central America would be that our funds were available to support "*voluntary* reintegration or *voluntary* regional relocation"[60] of the contras.

Sometimes, however, the power to persuade in diplomacy necessitates going well beyond mere word choice and must be backed up by "command presence." America's diplomatic relationship with the Chinese had been improving for almost two decades (since the days of Nixon-Kissinger) until the day the Chinese government decided to slaughter innocent citizens at Tiananmen Square on June 3, 1989. That homicidal act changed everything. President Bush, Secretary of State Baker, and every other American with a moral compass became more than outraged over the massacre, and Baker got to deliver America's high-intensity message face-to-face to Chinese ambassador Han Xu four days after the mass murder. Here's what former U.S. Marine James Baker, using his most forceful demonstra-

---

60. Ibid., 57.

tion of "command presence," told Ambassador Xu, again from *The Politics of Diplomacy*:

> "The President thought it would be a good idea for you to hear directly from me just how distressed he and I are over what is happening in your country," I told him. "The United States is committed to democracy and freedom of speech and assembly, and we cannot tolerate what we are seeing." I told him that the President expected the lives and property of American citizens to be protected, and that we wanted landing rights for American military planes based in Japan in order to evacuate American citizens on a moment's notice if required. "And I must remind you that while this President is a friend of China," I added, "the actions of your government cast a serious pall over our relations."[61]

From the moment Secretary of State Baker delivered his tough "read my lips" message, the Chinese understood that to the extent they ever wanted American cooperation on anything at all in the future, their acts of repression had to stop and never be repeated. They got the message.

Pragmatism and knowing when to drop one's guard. Just as James Baker had extended his philosophy of "principled pragmatism" from law to politics, he explained in his book how, as secretary of state, he saw immediately how the concept would work in guiding international diplomacy:

> In a sense, international politics can be thought of as an ongoing negotiation. I was taught that any complex negotiation was actually a series of discrete problems that required solutions. How you worked with the other side in developing the solution to the first problem had ramifications far beyond that single issue. Indeed, its resolution could set not just the logical precedents for subsequent issues, but the very tone of the relationship between the

---

61. Ibid., 106.

negotiators—and in the long run, that relationship could influence the course of events as much as any objective analysis of the points in dispute. If honesty and trust developed, even the most contentious talks could be brought to a successful conclusion. The negotiators feel free to set aside their formal negotiating positions and reveal their informal thinking—the assumptions, strategies, and even fears—that underlie their approach. Most often, I found when I could leave behind my formal brief and speak informally with my counterpart, success for both of us soon followed. But if the relationship soured—if it became infected with distrust and discord—then it mattered little how far apart the parties actually were. The perception of mistrust overwhelmed any objective reality.[62]

In particular, Baker used principled pragmatism and dropping his guard with the right person at the right time to foster harmonious relations between the United States and the Soviet Union, both before and after the Cold War ended, in the way he connected with foreign minister Eduard Shevardnadze. At first, they were international diplomatic counterparts; then as their formal relationship evolved, they began to trust each other as close friends. The Baker-Shevardnadze personal alliance became an essential component in the high-speed transformation of the countries' relationship, as it changed from confrontation to dialogue to collaboration on Baker's watch while he led the State Department.

Good timing. Baker's sense of "jugular timing" got used often during his time as secretary of state, as exemplified in the role he played in the international diplomatic process of unifying Germany. He recognized early on in his new position that "as location is to real estate, timing is to statecraft."[63] After the Berlin Wall fell on November 9, 1989, German unification had officially begun, but for it to succeed on all levels, Baker believed the best way to proceed was by implementing a policy he called "Two-plus-Four." Translated out of

---

62. Ibid., 134–135.

63. Ibid., 195.

shorthand, the policy meant that the best way for the two Germanys (East and West) to come together was for them to first resolve the internal issues between each side; then, after that had happened, the four nations who had occupied Germany after World War II— Britain, France, the Soviet Union, and the United States—would address the country's external issues as to how a unified Germany would best fit into the world order.

By Baker's living on airplanes to attend meetings all over Europe and Asia from January through mid-February 1990, pressing, pressing, pressing with focus, focus, focus to get an arrangement agreeable to all, while staying ahead of the actual unification activities that were going on at a breakneck speed inside Germany, and managing to get this accomplished at a time when the Soviet Union was trying to figure itself out as communism disintegrated, he miraculously succeeded (on an expedited basis) in overcoming objections by all interested parties about how best to achieve unification. Baker timed his diplomatic advances to the leaders of Germany and the other three participating countries so as to pressure one nation toward another until enough synergistic momentum built up to get all of them to sign off on Two-plus-Four in mid-February, which led to Baker's final desired result in October 1990: West Germany's annexing East Germany (the path chosen by the "Two") and the new Germany's becoming a member of both the European Community and NATO (the path chosen by the "Four").

Aversion to war until there's no other option. During George H. W. Bush's presidency, Iraq invaded Kuwait in August 1990, which led to the Gulf War. Immediately after the invasion, President Bush and Secretary of State Baker did everything in their powers to avoid the use of military power to reverse the invasion, but Iraq's leadership refused to respond to reason, sanctions, or anything else and took the hardline position that the only way they would ever vacate Kuwait would be by military force. How best to marshal that force? Bush and Baker both recognized that the only way to have complete success in the global arena in addressing Iraq's illegal invasion was for the United States to assemble an international coalition of military forces to attack and prevail over the Iraqi troops. The secretary of state accepted responsibility for pulling the laboring oar in building the thirty-four-country coalition that ultimately joined forces to triumph in Operation Desert Storm.

To build that coalition required Baker to lead the United Nations Security Council to authorize the use of military force for the first time since the Korean War, which he accomplished, in his words, through "an intricate process of cajoling, extracting, threatening, and occasionally buying votes. Such are the politics of diplomacy."[64] And when he was finished with that process (as he had always done in his battles with Congress during the Reagan years), James Baker obtained the requisite number of votes to win.

To get the Soviet vote at the UN Security Council, Baker became the first high-level American diplomat to ever visit the Russian equivalent of our Camp David. Thus, just as he had done as secretary of the treasury in lobbying Congress to support the Tax Reform Act of 1986, James Baker left the grandstands (of the State Department's offices in Washington, DC) and jumped into the middle of the international playing field wherever a game was being played and a score could lead to a vote at the United Nations.

After pocketing the necessary vote commitments, the time came for Chairman Baker to gavel the meeting of the UN Security Council to order on November 29, 1990. His description of that historic occasion in *The Politics of Diplomacy* is so compelling, only his words can do it justice:

> At 3:30 P.M., I gaveled the session to order. The chamber was packed, with galleries overflowing, and diplomats sitting and standing several deep around the conference table. It was the 2,963d meeting of the Security Council, and arguably the most important. Thirteen of the fifteen members were represented by their foreign ministers, only the fourth time in history the Council had convened at that level. I knew the votes were there, but I was speaking to a larger audience. The time had come to confront

---

64. Ibid., 305.

both Iraq *and* the American people with the proposition of war in the desert.

"I would like to begin today's discussion with a quotation that I think aptly sets the context for our discussions today," I said. "'There is . . . no precedent for a people being the victim of such injustice and of being at present threatened by abandonment to an aggressor. Also there has never before been an example of any government proceeding with the systematic extermination of a nation by barbarous means in violation of the most solemn promises, made to all the nations of the earth, that there should be no resort to a war of conquest and that there should not be used against innocent human beings terrible poison and harmful gases.'

"Those words could have come from the Emir of Kuwait, but they do not. They were spoken instead in 1936, not 1990. They come from Haile Selassie, the leader of Ethiopia, a man who saw his country conquered and occupied, much like Kuwait has been brutalized since August 2. Sadly, his appeal to the League of Nations fell upon deaf ears. The League's efforts to redress aggression failed, and international disorder and war ensued.

"History now has given us another chance. With the Cold War now behind us, we now have the chance to build the world envisioned by the founders of the United Nations. We have the chance to make this Security Council and this United Nations true instruments for peace and justice across the globe.

"We must not let the United Nations go the way of the League of Nations. We must fulfill our common vision of a peaceful and just post-Cold War world. But if we are to do so, we must meet the threat to international peace created by Saddam Hussein's aggression. That's why the debate we are about to begin will rank as one of the most important in the history of the United Nations. It will surely do much to determine the future of this body.

"Our aim today must be to convince Saddam Hussein that the just, humane demands of this council and the international community cannot be ignored. If Iraq does not reverse its course peacefully, then other necessary measures—including the use of force—should be authorized. We should put the choice to Saddam Hussein in unmistakable terms."[65]

Consistent with his approach as a prudent transactional lawyer wanting to avoid the businessperson's equivalent to war (i.e., civil litigation), Secretary of State Baker and President Bush made one final "last chance" effort to avoid engaging in the Gulf War, by scheduling a face-to-face meeting between Baker and Iraqi foreign minister Tariq Aziz in Geneva on January 9, 1991.

Using his best efforts at one-on-one persuasion at that meeting, the secretary of state opened with a dramatic flair, shaking hands with a stern look on his face in greeting Aziz and then delivering a sealed envelope containing a personal letter from President Bush to Saddam Hussein, asking the Iraqi foreign minister to play Baker's international power game, dance to his music, and take the letter to Aziz's leader. After handing over the envelope, Baker gave a "stark summation" of the global firepower that would rain down on Iraq's troops in the event of war, making it clear ("This isn't a threat, it's a promise"[66]) that Aziz's country was inviting a major military demonstration of force that would last only a few days (not weeks or months) before Iraqi troops would be pulverized, have to surrender, and withdraw in defeat from Kuwait. Next, Baker made it clear that the international coalition's demand for Iraq to pull out of Kuwait immediately was a nonnegotiable demand, and there were no other material terms to discuss. He also used carefully selected words (what Baker called "calculated ambiguity") to communicate the clear implication that if Iraq considered using chemical or biological warfare in any situation, then it would thereby invite nuclear retaliation (hardball anyone?). He closed his statement making it clear to Aziz

---

65. Ibid., 325–326.

66. James A. Baker, III. Speech to the World Affairs Council of Dallas/Fort Worth, Dallas, TX, November 2011.

that the thirty-four-country coalition had no problem allowing Iraq and Kuwait to resolve their differences on their own, but only after Iraq had withdrawn from Kuwait. His final words: "This is the last, best chance for peace."[67]

When nothing productive came from the "last chance" negotiation, the coalition's ground assault in the Gulf War lasted a grand total of one hundred hours, February 24–27, 1991, resulting in Iraq's troops retreating from Kuwait. In Baker's words, "The first test of the post–Cold War order had ended with American power and diplomacy triumphant."[68]

What was the historic significance of James Baker's time as secretary of state? He closed *The Politics of Diplomacy* with his answer to that question:

> As I reflect back now on my time as Secretary of State, I'm struck by my good fortune in occupying that office during a time of revolution, war, and peace: a revolution of freedom that swept away communism, a war of liberation that reversed a dictator's aggression, and progress toward peace, that established a foothold of reason in a region of enmity and conflict.
>
> That fortune is most clear when I look back over the world my predecessors were forced to navigate. From 1945 through 1989, eleven Secretaries of State steered America's way across a geopolitical map shaped by World War II and the Cold War. In three and one half years, those borders and boundaries were permanently redrawn. Indeed, the very nature of the international system as we had known it was transformed. . . .

---

67. Baker, *The Politics of Diplomacy*, 360.
68. Ibid., 410.

The world today is infinitely freer and safer than it has been during any other time in my life—and for that, I am grateful.[69]

———————

Following his time leading the State Department, James Baker served President George H. W. Bush as White House chief of staff for five months before leaving Washington. As a young man, James Baker had received gentle career counseling from his father to the effect that one advantage of being a lawyer was that "you will always have something to fall back on if other things fail."[70] Though he hadn't failed at anything during his time in Washington (except not always getting his presidential candidates elected), after leading President Bush's unsuccessful reelection campaign in 1992, Baker lived out his dad's advice and returned to Houston and "fell back" on the law firm that carried his DNA—Baker Botts—making him the fourth generation of his family to practice there. He told me, "It's great to get my ticket punched at the family firm."

In his almost two decades at Baker Botts, the firm has provided him with the best of all possible worlds: occupying a spacious corner office; working only on the jobs he chooses; avoiding the hassles of management responsibilities; taking on the high-level international diplomatic projects he selects at the request of the federal government; leading the James A. Baker, III Institute for Public Policy at Rice University; and *never* having to write down his billable time at the firm. James Baker received those perks the old-fashioned way: he earned them.

Baker took on a front-page responsibility in the public arena in November/December 2000. When the presidential election between Vice President Al Gore and Texas governor George W. Bush resulted in a disputed outcome because of uncertainty over the legitimacy of vote counts in Florida, litigation between the candidates arose to determine who would become the forty-third president of the United States.

———————

69. Ibid., 672.

70. James Baker, personal communication to author, June 28, 2011.

Gore aimed to put a "patina of statesmanship" spin on bringing his political lawsuit to challenge the election results in Florida, so he designated that the quarterback of his legal team handling the case would be former secretary of state Warren Christopher, who had served during the Clinton administration. Not to be outdone, Bush picked his own statesman, former secretary of state James Baker, to be his legal team's quarterback, and the litigation war was on, in which no settlement was possible.

As in all his past competitive encounters in life, James Baker didn't plan to be on the losing side of the case history remembers (because of the way it was styled at the United States Supreme Court) as *Bush v. Gore*. Whereas the micromanaging Gore never allowed Warren Christopher to call the plays on his case, Bush had the good sense to let superlawyer James Baker run his litigation show. Baker soon had under his direction what he considered to be the top trial and appellate lawyers in the country.

Though James Baker's days as a litigator were long gone, surrounded by the nation's top constitutional law scholars and advocates, his "proper preparation," "quick study" mind shifted into overdrive, and as the team quarterback, he gave network interviews while the lawsuits played themselves out and talked the litigation lingo as if he had done it his entire career:

> There's a rule of law to be followed in all elections. The state of Florida has established legal procedures to design, approve, publish, and if need be to protest ballots before the election. The [butterfly] ballot was designed by a Democratic elections supervisor. She approved it. The Democratic Party did not question it before the election. This butterfly-type ballot was used in recent elections in the same county and under the same rules and, again, the Democrats did not complain. . . . Our lawyers have confirmed the legality of this ballot. And we have with us here today . . . copies of the relevant Florida statutes if you would like to have them.[71]

---

71. Baker, *Work Hard*, 374–375.

In *Work Hard*, James Baker explained the exact magnitude of the Florida election litigation:

> The butterfly ballot cases illustrate what the rule of law is all about, which is playing by the rules as they existed *before* the game was played, then living with the results, good or bad. This is the same principle, by the way, that says you can't go to court to collect a debt if you file your lawsuit after the deadline set by the statute of limitations. It is unjust, in some sense, for a deadbeat debtor to get away without paying, but it would be an even greater injustice to change the rules after the event. The law is full of deadlines and technicalities and procedures, and if we purport to live under the rule of law, we have no choice but to respect them, even when they hurt us.[72]

Even though *Bush v. Gore* had important legal questions ultimately answered by the Supreme Court, there was precious little precedent to guide each of the courts in how to answer those questions. Baker explained the confluence of law and politics in the case:

> The case was 50 percent politics and 50 percent law. My counterpart, Warren Christopher, was a fine international lawyer in Los Angeles before he became secretary of state, but he was not really grounded in politics. We had to make arguments that were political in the various cases because there was no precedent to guide the courts. I got castigated by some Republicans for directing our lawyers to get our case into federal court because they claimed Republicans should always be in favor of states' rights. I answered that by asking the critics, "Do you want to win this thing or do you want to go with ideological principles?" This was certainly an example of principled pragmatism on my part.[73]

---

72. Ibid., 375.

73. James Baker, personal communication to author, June 28, 2011.

After all the lawsuits got filed, and all the hearings were held, Baker and his team succeeded in getting the case before the U.S. Supreme Court. There, in a 7-2 decision issued December 12, 2000, the nation's highest court held that the recount ordered by the Florida Supreme Court was unconstitutional because it involved counting rules that were not uniform, thereby violating the Constitution's equal-protection clause. With that holding, James Baker's client, George W. Bush, became the forty-third president of the United States.

When the litigation battle ended, Al Gore conceded defeat, and George W. Bush got sworn in as president. James Baker could essentially say about his Supreme Court success in *Bush v. Gore* what Leon Jaworski had said about his Supreme Court success in *U.S. v. Nixon*:

> Finally, the biggest lesson of Florida was that the system worked. Despite all the turmoil, as I told the foreign leaders, there were no riots and no tanks in the streets. We Americans may take the peaceful transfer of power for granted, but measured against the standards of history, Florida testifies to the strength of our constitutional democracy and our faith in the rule of law.[74]

CONCLUSION

Leon Jaworski functioned at a highly productive level until his sudden death at age seventy-seven, which occurred when he was chopping firewood on his ranch, while eighty-one-year-old James Baker will presumably still be firing on all cylinders at the time of this book's publication in early 2012. It would be a lost opportunity to detail these accomplished men's many historic achievements over extended periods of time, as detailed throughout this chapter, without noting the contrast in their lifestyles as compared to that of Theodore Roosevelt, whose lifestyle is detailed in chapter 4.

Immediately before his death at age sixty, Roosevelt was a burned-out, broken-hearted shell of a man who had thrown in

---

74. Baker, *Work Hard*, 390.

the towel on life and was ready to die. At age sixty, Leon Jaworski was fresh off his important work for the Justice Department in quashing the constitutional threat of Ross Barnett, the undisputed leader of a major law firm, and eight years away from accepting the position of Watergate special prosecutor. At that same age, James Baker was in his professional prime, changing the world for the better as President Bush's secretary of state. And ten years after that, Baker quarterbacked a team of superlawyers to victory in *Bush v. Gore*.

In the opinion of this writer, having researched the lives of all three men in preparing this book, primarily three factors account for the very different circumstances that arose for Roosevelt, Jaworski, and Baker upon arriving at age sixty. Rather than spoil the reader's enjoyment of chapter 4 by giving away in advance the delectable morsels of troubling information recited there about Theodore Roosevelt (thanks to the biographical scholarship of Edmund Morris, Douglas Brinkley, and Louis Auchincloss), this chapter closes by identifying the three common characteristics possessed by Jaworski and Baker at age sixty that allowed both of them to achieve their greatest professional heights upon entering their respective lives' seventh decade. The reader can later read chapter 4, make his own assessment of how Roosevelt measured up in the area of these characteristics, and determine whether his failure to possess them accounted for his physical and mental states immediately prior to his early death.

First, Jaworski and Baker had and have what it takes to develop and sustain long-term friendships—i.e., fundamentally consistent personalities marked by a logical flow of well-considered principled opinions that have allowed them to avoid burning bridges with their inner circles over the years. The torment of cognitive dissonance arising from internal conflict and contradictions has not been present in their lives, which makes possible one's being able to pursue convictions with a long-term support team and not incur the heartburn that arises when friends turn into foes.

Second, Messrs. Jaworski and Baker have maintained an awareness of the importance in recharging one's batteries on a regular basis when pursuing lives filled with high stress, tackling major challenges, and encountering frequent drama. Both men found and regularly used their getaway retreats, where they could relax and clear the mind to allow for reflection and physical exercise—Leon Jaworski at his Hill Country ranch outside Wimberley, Texas, and James Baker at his Wyoming ranch south of Jackson Hole. For them to have pressed on nonstop with their busy careers, with high intensity month after month, year after year, would have caused their minds and inner machinery to deteriorate and soon wear out long before their warranty period had expired.

Last but not least, Jaworski and Baker looked to a higher power on a regular basis, knowing that the person who lives each day in a mode of believing in his self-sufficiency absorbs a burden that produces ever-enhancing fatigue.

Early in his final book, *Crossroads*, Leon Jaworski recounts the wisdom his minister father delivered to him shortly after his mother's death when he was a young boy, which stayed with him throughout his life: "None of the good things we try to do will last. Only the love we give others for the sake of God endures forever."[75] He closes the book arriving at a miraculous level of internal serenity in the context of processing the tragedy of losing two beloved grandsons, seven years apart, in motor vehicle accidents while both were still young men. In that overwhelming circumstance of the deepest sorrow, the greatest American litigator of the last half century spoke of how he viewed his future and then closed with the words of former United Nations secretary general Dag Hammarskjold:

> Now as I enter my seventy-fifth year, I know there will be more crossroads to come. With the Lord's guidance and support, I will do my best to meet them. And whatever happens, I can only pray:
> "For all that has been, thanks. To all that shall be, yes."[76]

James Baker spent the first part of his career as a lawyer in Houston avoiding church and following in his father's footsteps as a

---

75. Jaworski, *Crossroads*, 19.
76. Ibid., 216.

bona fide workaholic. Inspired by the deep faith of his second wife, Susan, Baker's faith became a work in progress until he reached a level of comfort in his faith that he could discuss it in men's groups and prayer breakfasts; proclaim its power in his autobiography, *Work Hard*; and minister to his own family, as Susan recounted in her book, *Passing It On*. Here is Susan Baker's account of a family reunion religious service he led in August 2007:

> Jim gave a short, powerful talk about letting God be God, not trying to play God ourselves.
>
> Speaking especially to the grandchildren, Jim said that early on he thought he had to do it all by himself. He should be independent, strong, he thought, not needing or depending on others. Then he found out he was wrong. In fact, he did need God. And he needed other people in his life—most of all, his family.[77]

In *Work Hard*, James Baker provided the reading public with the following explanation for the importance of faith in his life:

> Many believe faith is more difficult for those in public life. For me, at least, the exact opposite was true. Living in the centrifuge of politics encouraged, even demanded, spiritual growth. That life was certainly exciting and, in many ways, satisfying. But power can also be intoxicating and addictive. "Power tends to corrupt, and absolute power corrupts absolutely," Lord Acton said, and I think that's true. I've felt the temptation myself, and it's unsettling.
>
> In addition, temporal power is fleeting. I cleaned out my desk in January 1993 and became a private citizen. Like the lonely chief of staff I had spotted on Pennsylvania Avenue so many years before, all my titles now had "former" in front of them. As my public prominence diminished, I also discovered that I could stand on busy street corners and walk through airports without being

---

77. Baker, *Passing It On* (Houston, TX: Bright Sky Press, 2010), 15.

recognized. This was liberating in a way, but also—truth be told—disquieting.

Power has its satisfactions, but inner security and the deepest kind of personal fulfillment are not among them. It is only through a relationship with God, not by our actions here on earth, that life has real meaning. And for me, at least, a life of faith does not come easily. I have to work at it.[78]

The reader is invited to keep all of chapter 2 in mind, and particularly its conclusion, as he reads chapter 4. If we cannot learn lessons that have application for our own daily lives from studying the experiences of famous men and women, then why bother to read biographies at all?

---

78. Baker, *Work Hard*, 413.

CHAPTER THREE

The Lawyer as Novelist: Opening the Public's Mind to a New Perspective

A lawyer frustrated with his career, dependent on the mundane matters in his inbox to supply his daily challenges, often dreams of doing "something else." The dream fades for most, however, when no alternative career enters the imagination likely to match the attorney's income.

For a few though, brainstorming soon ramps up on the dream, and the lawyer (particularly the trial lawyer) recognizes that yes, he does possess the skills as a storyteller needed to sway the fact finder, and yes, he also has the skills as a writer capable of persuading judges. Wait a second! Storyteller + writer = novelist! By golly, there is a way out of this billable hour, "the client is always right" drudgery!

Sometimes, as in the cases of Louis Auchincloss, Richard North Patterson, and John Grisham, the dream comes true and the reading public becomes the beneficiary.

Facing page: Louis Auchincloss. Photographer: Frank Capri. Photo courtesy of Getty Images.

LOUIS AUCHINCLOSS

The epiphany resulting from the alternative-career meditation materialized first for Louis Auchincloss, the trailblazer of the successful lawyer-novelist path.[1] As a thirty-year-old associate at the Wall Street firm of Sullivan & Cromwell, Auchincloss had his novel *The Indifferent Children* published in 1947 by Prentice-Hall. He had written the book during the final months of his military service, and his fearful mother (concerned that the book wasn't very good) and his fearful father (concerned that his son's employer might react unfavorably to the book) insisted that he use a pseudonym for the work. The secret didn't last long.

No worries. His law firm's management accepted Auchincloss's writing avocation as long as he fulfilled his work responsibilities and wrote about nothing likely to cause problems with clients or his fellow lawyers. The young attorney surely winced, though, at the response by senior partner John Foster Dulles made shortly after the book's release, to the charge that he was running a sweatshop for young attorneys: "On the contrary," the future secretary of state said, "the associates have to fill out the day writing novels."[2] The secret no longer a secret, Auchincloss's pseudonym vanished after the first book.

In May of 1947, *The Indifferent Children* received a glowing review from William McFee, a respected author of the era, who compared Auchincloss to celebrated novelist Henry James. In his autobiography, Auchincloss wrote that McFee's public assessment boosted his self-confidence and clarified to the young attorney that he should keep writing fiction.

Enjoying the independence gained from earning a respectable paycheck at a prominent firm, and hooked (after McFee's affirmation of his talent) on writing fiction whenever his schedule permitted (early mornings, nights, weekends, and the rare dead time at the office), Auchincloss practiced law *and* wrote novels and short stories

---

1. The facts of Auchincloss's life described in this chapter come from his memoir, *A Writer's Capital* (Minneapolis: University of Minnesota Press, 1974), and the superb biography *Louis Auchincloss: A Writer's Life* (New York: Crown, 1993), written by Carol Gelderman.

2. Gelderman, *Louis Auchincloss*, 111.

for the next four years, achieving a level of success on both fronts. Believing, however, that he could never emerge from the pack in either field as long as he split his focus, Auchincloss decided double-decking his career was unsustainable. With his father's financial support, he left Sullivan & Cromwell to become a full-time writer at the end of 1951.

During his sabbatical from the law, Auchincloss wrote constantly. More important to his ultimate career path, through successful psychotherapy, he achieved a genuine belief in himself. But after almost three years away from the practice of law, he concluded that (1) his singular focus on writing had not improved its quantity or quality, (2) as a lifestyle, he greatly preferred supporting himself on a lawyer's salary (instead of being financially dependent on his parents), and (3) he liked filling his days with intellectual and social engagement at a busy law firm in the company of colleagues whose friendship he enjoyed (as opposed to enduring the solitary existence of a professional writer).

Upon reaching this conclusion, as the master of his own destiny, Auchincloss confidently resumed his dual career in law and literature, pursuing both vocations unconflicted and unafraid. He no longer tried to classify himself as being of either one or the other profession, which he considered a positive step in his personal development.

Picking up his practice as a trust and estate specialist in 1953, and prohibited from rejoining Sullivan & Cromwell (because of their policy prohibiting the hiring of boomerang lawyers), Auchincloss joined the white shoe New York firm of Hawkins, Delafield, & Wood, where, after making partner in 1958, he stayed the remainder of his legal career.

Being a lawyer in the nation's financial nerve center had a positive impact on Auchincloss's success as a professional writer, which he readily acknowledged:

- "Four decades of the practice of law on Wall Street brought me close to the pulse of our legal and financial systems, both notoriously neglected by American novelists often sheltered in universities."

- "I think my practice in law has enhanced my writing in providing all kinds of thoughts, ideas, and inspirations; and of course I've written a good deal about the law."
- "I think [practicing law] is a profession ideally married to writing because both deal with the written word and an emphatic need for probing and analyzing."
- "The importance of English to the lawyer amount[s] almost to a religion."[3]

Unlike lawyer-novelists Richard North Patterson and John Grisham (whose careers are detailed later in this chapter), Louis Auchincloss was never a trial lawyer, staying away from an area of the law that biographer Carol Gelderman says would have made it difficult to maintain dual careers:

> Louis contented himself with his place in trusts and estates, which was not deadline work and rarely kept him late at the office, enabling him to keep writing—and by this time he was writing at the office every chance he got.[4]

In addition to the scheduling benefit, the trust and estate law practice at his Wall Street law firm provided the ideal environment for Auchincloss's fertile imagination to reach new heights as he spent his days advising clients on how to preserve their wealth. His novels' characters and plots always swirled in the upper-class realm of New York City, meaning his settings included prep schools, private clubs, debutante parties, brownstone apartments, summer homes, established law firms, powerful financial institutions, and showplace residences of families estranged over the distribution of inheritance. In this world of the silk stocking elite, tension abounded but there were few lawsuits, which suited nonlitigator Louis Auchincloss's storytelling just fine.

---

3. These four quotes are taken from Gelderman's *Louis Auchincloss*, 169, 174, 191, 182.

4. Ibid., 115.

Without trial experience, and inhabiting a society largely averse to litigation, when Auchincloss wrote about law in his fiction, his plots understandably didn't include courtroom battles; rather, he created stories that explored "the rich untapped areas of the inner working of the big law firm and its clients." According to Auchincloss, "What goes on within the lawyer's office is . . . packed with drama. I have always found that this field makes for the quickest writing as the stories seem to write themselves."[5]

Biographer Gelderman amplified her subject's words:

> Auchincloss's legal stories confirm what outsiders have always believed about Wall Street lawyers, namely that money is all-important. Lawyers, after all, serve a society that is bent on making money. . . . A fictional lawyer is a useful foil for exploring moral restraints of such an ethic because a lawyer is paid to be an energetic servant of and not moral auditor of his clients' interests. . . .
>
> Most of Louis Auchincloss's legal stories are gems of irony, ambivalence, ambiguity, metaphor: all techniques by means of which two or more views of experience may be expressed simultaneously. How else could he so vividly embody the inherent difficulties of occupying, as lawyers do, a unique position within society, for they are located on the boundary between clients and the law, between private and public interests.[6]

With a clear head (from successful psychotherapy) and practicing at the right law firm whose partners enjoyed having a prominent novelist in the midst of their daily lives, Louis Auchincloss's writing career took off in the 1960s. During that decade, as Ms. Gelderman summarizes, he wrote "five novels, three books of essays, two books of short stories"—and in that mix was nominated for the Pulitzer Prize and the National Book Award and had "four book-club selections, five best-sellers, four front-page reviews in *The New York Times Book Review*," and articles published regularly in America's

---

5. Ibid., 182–183.
6. Ibid., 188, 191.

leading newspapers and magazines.[7] With this prodigious level of productivity, Auchincloss reached the point where he told his friend Gore Vidal that he made "as much money from writing as from the law"[8]—no small feat, given his status as a partner at one of the most profitable law firms in the country at that time.

What caused Louis Auchincloss's fiction devoted to the lives of New York City's upper crust to achieve such meteoric success in the turbulent 1960s? Gore Vidal answered the question in a 1974 interview:

> The world Auchincloss writes about, the domain of Wall Street bankers and lawyers and stockbrokers, is thought to be irrelevant, a faded and fading genteel-gentile en- clave when, in actual fact, this little world comprises the altogether too vigorous and self-renewing ruling class of the United States—an oligarchy that is in firm control of the Chase Manhattan Bank, American foreign policy, and the decision-making processes of both divisions of the Property Party.[9]

According to Vidal, Auchincloss was the only novelist at that time writing about such a realm and about the role of money in people's lives.

Though Auchincloss left the practice of law in 1986 at the age of sixty-nine because of his firm's mandatory retirement policy, he continued to write at a brisk pace until his death in January 2010. By the end of his career, he had authored over sixty books, which included thirty-one novels, seventeen nonfiction works (made up in part by his memoir and five biographies), and seventeen short story collections. Among the significant honors bestowed on Auchincloss in recognition of his body of work were his being named a Fellow by the American Academy of Arts and Letters, being recognized as a "Living Landmark" by the New York Landmarks Conservancy

7. Ibid., 167.
8. Ibid.
9. Ibid., 169.

in 2000, and receiving the National Medal of Arts from President George W. Bush in 2005.

Louis Auchincloss's success established a precedent for the next generation of lawyer-novelists to thrive as they mined their mother lode imaginations. The rest of this chapter is devoted to two of Auchincloss's successors, Richard North Patterson and John Grisham, who (in the opinion of this attorney-writer) have "raised the bar" in broadening society's bandwidth through the impact of their books, which have been devoured by the masses for the last two decades.

Carol Gelderman notes in her biography of Auchincloss, "the first principle of good writing, one he takes seriously, is to entertain."[10] Her subject consistently satisfied that principle and never aspired to write books aimed at changing the world; rather, Auchincloss sought to entertain his readers by enlightening them about the hearts, minds, souls, conflicts, anxieties, and tensions of the big city power elite. Richard North Patterson and John Grisham, on the other hand, have had a different mission in their writing. Though they began their literary careers achieving success as best-selling authors fully committed to entertaining readers by engaging them in riveting plots built around law, crime, and courtroom drama, upon selling several million books and achieving extraordinary financial success, they independently made the decision to expand the scope of their novels to address social, legal, and political issues, though these stories are still filled with heightened suspense and keep the multitudes turning their pages at breakneck speed.

RICHARD NORTH PATTERSON

Unlike Louis Auchincloss, Richard North Patterson had no desire to write novels when he first became a lawyer. Following his 1971 graduation from Case Western Reserve Law School, Patterson began his career in the regulatory arena, prosecuting fraud as an

---

10. Ibid., 164.

assistant attorney general for the state of Ohio and then pursuing enforcement claims and investigating the Watergate scandal for the Securities and Exchange Commission in Washington, DC. After that stint as a government lawyer, he engaged in private practice as a civil litigator at law firms in Birmingham and San Francisco.

The moment of truth, when Patterson determined that his career would have to involve something more than being a lawyer, came while working on a case in Birmingham that required him to take multiple out-of-town trips in rapid succession to satisfy a judge's heavy-handed accelerated discovery order. The constant travel disconnected him for extended periods from his one-year-old son. On an airplane after leaving home one too many times, depressed by the memory of his young boy's waving good-bye, Patterson asked himself, "Why am I doing this?" and "What else can I do to make a living to support my family besides be a lawyer?"

Seeking answers to those questions brought an immediate result. At that point in his life, Patterson had been consuming a steady diet of Ross Macdonald's mystery novels. From that, he believed he had grasped the rudimentary elements of writing fiction (i.e., point of view and linear plotting). So while on the plane, in taking the first step toward a new career, he roughed out a plot for a novel and, later that night, began writing the first chapter.

Patterson soon recognized his limitations as a novice writer and decided he needed formal instruction. When his business trips became less frequent, he enrolled in an introductory writing class at the University of Alabama at Birmingham, and his work product was deemed good enough to warrant his selection to study there with accomplished Southern fiction writer Jesse Hill Ford.

Under Ford's guidance, Patterson's writing improved to the point of his getting a short story published in *Atlantic Monthly*, followed by the publication of his first suspense thriller, *The Lasko Tangent* (New York: W.W. Norton & Co., 1979), which was selected by the Mystery Writers of America in 1980 as an Edgar Allan Poe Award

---

Facing page: Richard North Patterson. Photo courtesy of Miranda Lewis.

winner for being that year's best first novel by an American author.

Though the advance and royalties from *The Lasko Tangent* weren't enough to allow Patterson to quit his day job, with the release of his second mystery, *The Outside Man* (New York: Ballantine Books, 1981), he believed he was on the road to financial security with his writing. The budding novelist resigned from his Birmingham law firm, moved to the West Coast, and for the next four years produced two more works of fictional crime and intrigue, which met with critical acclaim but underwhelming sales. Patterson realized that his dream of supporting his family solely as a writer was not materializing, so he returned to practicing law in 1985. Joining the San Francisco office of what is now the Bingham-McCutchen law firm, Patterson resumed his career as a full-time commercial litigator for the next eight years, made partner there, and in 1993 earned the right to a three-month sabbatical from the firm.

But as he began his sabbatical, the stars had realigned. Something fortuitous for Patterson occurred in American fiction between 1985 and 1993, as he billed time, took depositions, and tried cases for his San Francisco firm. Chicago-based criminal lawyer Scott Turow had his first novel, *Presumed Innocent*, published in 1987; it hit #1 on the *New York Times* bestseller list and in 1990 became a blockbuster movie starring Harrison Ford. Then Mississippi sole practitioner John Grisham's second novel, *The Firm*, sold several million copies, became the best-selling book in the country for 1991, and was quickly turned into a successful film featuring Tom Cruise. All of a sudden, the "legal thriller" genre was the rage, and major publishers looked in earnest for other lawyer-novelists who could produce fiction and turn it to gold like Turow and Grisham.

Seizing the opportunity during the sabbatical from his law firm, Patterson speed-wrote *Degree of Guilt* in ninety days, and Ballantine Books immediately published it. Soon, it became his first novel to make the *New York Times* bestseller list, was produced into an NBC TV miniseries, and received the French Grand Prix de Litterature Policiere Award. Patterson believed his ship as an author had come in (at last!), obtained a six-month unpaid leave of absence from his law firm to write his next novel, and then got a big enough advance for his next two books to leave his legal career behind in 1993 and never return.

Richard North Patterson felt like he had won the lottery. In his words, what occurred to him in 1993 was

> a coincidental merger of a natural subject for me to write about—the law—with the arrival in the book-buying marketplace of a desire to read novels by lawyers who could tell a compelling story. Success was as accidental as being hit by a moon rock, but a whole lot more fun.[11]

From 1994 to 1997, Patterson produced four suspense novels full of criminal conduct, investigations, and trials, and all of them made the bestseller list. With each book, his fan club grew. One of his most devoted readers became former president George H. W. Bush, who was so impressed with Patterson's work that he sent the author a fan letter, which ultimately transformed his career. Seizing potential opportunity, Patterson replied to the former president with a note expressing his appreciation for the fan letter, and he let his new admirer know that what he really wanted to write thrillers about in his future novels was politics, aspiring to be his generation's Allen Drury, whose book *Advise and Consent* won the Pulitzer Prize for fiction in 1960. At the time he sent the note to President Bush, Patterson knew no one who could open the door for him into the world of presidential politics, and he believed that writing with credibility about how those in the upper echelons of national power operate would require access to the people in high political places. So Patterson asked his fan to introduce him to the former president's vast network of influential people in furtherance of pursuing a new genre for his future novels.

To the writer's surprise, Bush agreed and then followed through. Patterson gained expertise from President Bush's introductions, which allowed him to write his next bestseller, *No Safe Place* (New York: Alfred A. Knopf, 1998), with a plot involving an attempted presidential assassination by an abortion protestor. The author dedi-

---

11. Richard North Patterson, personal communication to author, May 16, 2011.

cated the book to the person who had made it possible: George H. W. Bush.

Once the political door opened for Richard North Patterson, it never closed. From the mid-1990s through the present, he has substantially expanded his network of political relationships in both the Republican and Democratic parties and used the knowledge and access gained to produce subsequent novels involving the most controversial national and international political issues of the last decade.

I had the opportunity to critique *Protect and Defend* (New York: Alfred A. Knopf, 2000), his first major political thriller after *No Safe Place*, for the *Dallas Morning News*. My 2001 review, reprinted below, attempts to explain how Patterson rose to the challenge of raising his platform as a novelist by "tackling the abortion behemoth."[12]

More than nine years ago, John Grisham and Scott Turow kicked off the trend of lawyers becoming best-selling fiction writers. Since then, other lawyers have produced commercially successful suspense novels, but Richard North Patterson moves to the head of the class with *Protect and Defend*.

Unlike his competitors, Mr. Patterson has resisted the urge to churn out one formulaic murder mystery after another. With his new book, the former Ohio assistant attorney general attempts to wrap his arms around the moral and political issue of abortion, examining his subject through voices of both abortion rights advocates and abortion rights opponents.

The plot adds voltage to the word *spellbinding*. Kerry Kilcannon becomes president after a race too close to call on election night. Seconds after his inaugural address, the chief justice of the U.S. Supreme Court drops dead from

12. Talmage Boston, "Tackling the Abortion Behemoth," *Dallas Morning News*, January 28, 2001. Reprinted with permission of the *Dallas Morning News*.

a heart attack, leaving a 4-4 split on the court between liberals and conservatives.

The new chief executive knows his choice to fill the vacancy will be highly scrutinized, especially the nominee's stance on abortion. As the selection process begins, a landmark case is filed challenging the constitutionality of the Protection of Life Act: The 15-year-old plaintiff is five months pregnant, and her sonogram shows a hydrocephalic fetus. Delivery at term would require a special C-section that may result in her permanent infertility.

The teenager's lawyer, an associate with a big firm who does pro bono counseling at an abortion clinic, is only three years removed from clerking for the Ninth Circuit justice who becomes President Kilcannon's Supreme Court nominee. The nominated female judge has a secret daughter (adopted at birth by her sister) whom she chose not to abort some 20 years earlier. The president's fiancée and the daughter of the Senate Judiciary Committee chairman both have had undisclosed abortions.

As a former trial lawyer himself, Mr. Patterson knows that only exhaustive research can build a novel on the complex topics of judicial confirmation, late-term abortion litigation, the media's role in exposing private lives of public figures, and the power of money in today's political arena. The author interviewed former presidents Bush and Clinton and federal judges, senators, and experts on both sides of the abortion question for this timely, authentic story.

Mr. Patterson's stated goal for *Protect and Defend* is for it to do for the abortion issue what Jerome Lawrence's drama *Inherit the Wind* did for the creation-evolution debate. On the abortion question, for which there appears to be no compromise position, the Supreme Court nominee has to acknowledge privately that "there is much to be said on either side." Her sentiments are not unique. When asked his reaction to the competing arguments given to the Ninth Circuit, President Kilcannon replies, "I was re-calling why I have such mixed feelings about all of this."

During his prior legal career, like all good lawyers, Patterson recognized the necessity of analyzing all aspects of his and his op-ponent's case, and he did exactly the same thing with the abortion debate in *Protect and Defend*. Three years later, his next bestseller, *Balance of Power* (New York: Ballantine Books, 2003), addressed the national debate on gun control. Again, he wanted to write a book that would explain all sides of a controversial political issue. His research, however, was restricted by the National Rifle Association's (NRA) refusal to have any of their leaders interviewed by the au-thor. Perhaps such interviews with the NRA's spokespersons would have given Patterson some new insight into their uncompromising position on the "right to bear arms" that he would have worked into the story. Perhaps not. We'll never know. My 2003 review of *Balance of Power*, reprinted below, made it clear that the book reflected the work of a highly skilled advocate, now taking his powers of persuasion outside the courtroom and into the national political arena, who had had his fill of the NRA's tunnel vision perspective on the Second Amendment's giving every fanatic in America the right to own a high-powered gun in the context of too many mass homicides.[13]

Does the Second Amendment's "right to bear arms" guarantee a citizen the right to own a 40-shot magazine assault weapon without going through a pre-purchase background check? The National Rifle Association says "yes." Richard North Patterson's new 600-page thriller says "no."

---

13. Talmage Boston, "Mystery Puts NRA in the Line of Fire," *Dallas Morning News*, November 23, 2003. Reprinted with permission of the *Dallas Morning News*.

Gun control has become a boiling-point issue in politics and litigation alike. And Mr. Patterson turns up the heat.

A lawyer until his murder mysteries started landing on best-seller lists, Mr. Patterson stepped into the world of fictional political intrigue five years ago, aided by a fan club of national leaders (former presidents George H. W. Bush and Bill Clinton, Senate leaders Bob Dole and Ted Kennedy) who educated the author on the inner workings of the federal government. His books *No Safe Place* and *Protect and Defend* examined the abortion question while touching on other issues in the headlines. *Balance of Power* completes the trilogy with the author's spin on the politics of guns.

The book sustains multiple interwoven tales—sibling rivalry, family physical abuse, mass murder, political corruption, blackmail, legislative battles, courtroom drama, a love story, religious extremism, media intrusion—with every character having a fair share of closet skeletons.

With its tight, bullet-like quip approach to the gun debate, *Balance of Power* should mow down any doubts that the pen rules. Though the NRA wants criminals prosecuted to the full extent of the law, "Will they also resurrect the victims?" Should "the life of a 6-year-old mass murder target outweigh the right of a madman to buy any gun he wants?" In his research, the author interviewed representatives from every organization weighing in on gun control except the NRA, which he says rejected his many requests for a meeting.

Perhaps the strongest point of the book comes when the Senate Majority Leader, a tool of the gun lobby, finally gets his fill of the NRA chairman's opposition to making guns subject to consumer protection laws because "it would be the first step toward ending gun rights in America."

The senator snaps at his political godfather: "Everything is the first step. By your logic, the income tax is the first step to confiscating our money, and the death penalty the first step to Nazi crematoriums. Has it ever dawned on you that society stands on a continuum, not poised on a slippery slope?"

Balance of Power is no holiday gift for the NRA, but it should work for the thoughtful reader concerned about the staggering number of gun homicides in America.

Patterson followed *Balance of Power* with *Conviction* (New York: Random House, 2005), a novel about the national debate on capital punishment. A short excerpt from my 2005 review of *Conviction* shows that Patterson was back into the mode of telling a great story while fully exploring the many angles of this moral, legal, and political issue:[14]

> Mr. Patterson leaves no legal or political stone unturned in his examination of both sides of the death penalty issue. Along the way, he delivers vivid settings and dialogues from the crime, investigation, trial and appeals all the way to the U.S. Supreme Court and execution. The quality and thoroughness of each event's description in this tight jurisprudential timeline is so flawless that *Conviction* should become required reading for every American law student.
>
> As *Conviction* shows, critical questions often have no clear answers. At what level of mental incapacity should our courts change the rules for a criminal defendant's trial? What amount of attorney malpractice should entitle a Death Row felon to a new trial? But the ultimate question in *Conviction* is: Should the main goal of post-conviction litigation be achieving finality or preventing the potential execution of innocent people?

---

14. Talmage Boston, "Death Penalty Case Is Far from Closed," *Dallas Morning News*, March 27, 2005. Reprinted with permission of the *Dallas Morning News*.

After *Conviction*, Patterson addressed the many political issues that could come up during a modern-era presidential campaign in *The Race* (New York: Henry Holt & Company, 2007). In the book's acknowledgments, he listed some of those issues, which include the uneasy alliance between business interests and religious conservatives, the politicization of science, how political polarization has negatively impacted governance and public policy, how our system of campaign finance has become corrupt, how our political dialogue has become dominated by a cynical marketing mentality, and how Americans continue to find it difficult to honestly confront race.

The author then clearly stated his opinion that contemporary politics as practiced are accelerating America's decline. According to Patterson, the majority of Americans long for authentic leaders who will tell the truth and who care more about the country than promoting themselves and creating further distrust and discord.

Richard North Patterson thereby spoke for virtually all Americans in expressing his total disgust with contemporary politics. Most of us, however, merely grumble about politics and do nothing to effect a change in a broken system. This lawyer-novelist stepped up to the plate and swung for the fences with a persuasive story calculated to affect reasonable minds on how contemporary politics needs to change.

Ever evolving, Patterson entered the international political arena with his next two novels. *Exile* (New York: Henry Holt & Company, 2007) attempts to grasp the most pertinent elements in the competing philosophical, political, and military battles waged in the Israeli-Palestinian conflict and allowed the author to bring his flair for courtroom dramatics back into his plots. Next came *Eclipse* (New York: Henry Holt & Company, 2009), a novel about an African nation and how international dependence on oil disrupts every aspect of the society. This novel also has a climactic courtroom scene, based on an actual trial that took place in Nigeria, where Patterson educates the reader about the "Kafkaesque perversion of the forms of justice"[15] in modern Africa.

---

15. "Author Talk," accessed May 9, 2011, http://www.bookreporter.com/authors/richard-north-patterson/news/talk-011609.

Patterson's most recent novels, *In the Name of Honor* (New York: Henry Holt & Company, 2010) and *The Devil's Light* (New York: Scribner, 2011) deal respectively with the front page subjects of the effect of post-traumatic stress disorder on our returning American soldiers and al Qaeda's ways, means, and ultimate intentions. They continue his streak of books over the last decade that expand readers' awareness of complex issues, dramatizing questions that have no simple answers, which confront our country and our world every single day.

In his interviews, Patterson explains how he views his emerging role as a writer who attempts to enlighten readers on an ever-expanding scope of political issues, bringing clarity on the strengths and weaknesses of his subjects' points in conflict:

- "The work of a novelist involves one of the most important ingredients of a civilized society: the written word—the work of disparate people from countless different backgrounds, which nonetheless illuminates our common humanity."[16]

- "I can only write a novel as if it matters, hopeful that if I care about a subject, others will as well. I do know that I've changed individual minds, and caused readers to look at some of our most visceral controversies in a different way. I also believe that when any individual speaks out—including a novelist—it sends ripples throughout a society."[17]

- "If I had just kept writing about jury trials in suspense thrillers, it would have driven me crazy. I gained inside knowledge about the political world through my friendships with Presidents George H. W. Bush and Bill Clinton, Secretary of Defense Bill Cohen, Secretary of State Hillary Clinton, Senators Ted Kennedy, John McCain, and Barbara Boxer, so why not use it? If you don't set challenges, you run the risk of boring yourself and boring the reader."[18]

---

16. "Interview with Richard North Patterson," accessed May 9, 2011, http://www.panmacmillan .com/interviews/displayPage.asp?PageID=5461.

17. "Interview with Richard North Patterson," accessed May 9, 2011, http://thethrillerguy .blogspot.com/2010/02/richard-north-patterson.html.

18. Richard North Patterson, personal communication to author, May 16, 2011.

- "I do my best to present all sides of an issue. If I don't do that, my political fiction would be mere propaganda. I recognize that those with different opinions than me on issues hold their views in good faith, have substance to back their beliefs, and have ethical dignities in their positions. It would be intellectually dishonest for me not to acknowledge that in my novels."[19]

- "In writing novels about complex political issues, I am not only in the entertainment business; I am also in the education business—attempting to give the reader the components he needs to form a well-considered opinion on an issue."[20]

In a personal interview I conducted with Richard North Patterson in May of 2011, he acknowledged that, for a number of reasons, he could not have executed the high-impact political novels he's written had he never been a trial lawyer. First, most of his political thrillers have had a trial or an appeal as a focal point in their plots, which he says is a natural thing, recognizing that "some of our great political and social controversies have been decided by courts—*Brown v. Board of Education* and *Roe v. Wade* come to mind immediately." His gift for creating electrifying courtroom battles in almost every one of his books comes from his experience as a litigator who understood trial dynamics and knew how to question a witness to get the right answers. In addition, as only someone who's been both a fiction writer and a trial lawyer knows, every successful novel had better sizzle with conflict, and the courtroom is often the best place to level the playing field for competing positions.

Second, just as a lawyer must wrap his brain around all pertinent facts and law in his case (both favorable and unfavorable), the political novelist seeking to open and expand the public mind-set on a controversial subject must do the same. He told me, "Only by attempting to fully educate oneself about an issue can a citizen determine how he or she should feel—otherwise, the opinion formed

---

19. Ibid.
20. Ibid.

is prejudiced by incomplete information, which I definitely want to avoid."

Third, both the successful trial lawyer and novelist must tell engaging stories that make sense. According to Patterson, "I do my damnedest to give readers what's at the root of the conflict on both sides, and presenting facts on all sides of the issues in an intelligible way." In addition, the person creating the literary drama has the responsibility to "keep his presentation entertaining or else his readers will close the book, just as the litigator has the job of keeping the fact finder alert or else he'll daydream or go to sleep." As another essential element in the successful storytelling process, the trial lawyer attempts to understand and orchestrate witnesses' strengths and weaknesses, and the novelist does the same to maximize the vividness of the characters he creates.

Finally, a trial lawyer in high-stakes litigation learns to rely on expert witnesses to understand complicated situations and with that also knows how to penetrate an expert's analysis when it's flawed. In writing each of his political thrillers, Patterson interviews approximately one hundred experts who have differing opinions on the subjects his books address. Only by engaging in such a thorough process can the author have confidence that his arms have fully encircled his chosen area of focus, allowing him to create accurate settings, believable characters, and authentic plots as he explores the conflicted issues about which he writes.

Apart from religious considerations, the goal of every human being should be to use his most consequential talents to maximize his potential while operating in a mode of uncompromising integrity. Richard North Patterson's life exemplifies that goal. Fully utilizing every aspect of the skills he developed as a trial lawyer for the better part of twenty years, he has given his best shot at attempting to make his mark in the world (and not just the literary world) as a best-selling writer who, using fiction, takes on our most controversial social, legal, and political issues more comprehensively and with more intellectual honesty than any politician or media commentator could ever hope to achieve. Undoubtedly, he would have sold more books if he had stuck solely with crime mysteries, but to do that would have put him in conflict with achieving his higher purpose as a writer—to produce novels that open readers' minds to better understand the national and international conflicts around them and therefore potentially change lives.

JOHN GRISHAM

Last in this chapter's trilogy is John Grisham, whose success as a lawyer-novelist is second to none. Through 2011, his twenty-five books published in twenty-two years have been translated into over thirty languages and have sold more than 250 million copies. Nine of his novels have been produced into major motion pictures (and one into a made-for-TV movie), *A Time to Kill* became a Broadway play in 2011, and, in January 2012, NBC began airing a television series based on *The Firm*.

Though the books that made him rich and famous were high-entertainment legal thrillers, in the last decade, Grisham has expanded his repertoire and shown he's no one-trick pony, writing bestsellers outside his specialty, which include a semiautobiographical work about his childhood on an Arkansas cotton farm (*A Painted House*); a Christmas story (*Skipping Christmas*); a sports drama (*Bleachers*); a tale of "What's life really about?" (*Playing for Pizza*); a nonfiction book (*The Innocent Man*); a movie screenplay (*Mickey*); a short story collection (*Ford County*); and the start of a children's mystery series featuring protagonist Theo Boone, "kid lawyer." Through creating an enviable track record of producing one blockbuster book after another for more than two decades, between the ages of thirty-four and fifty-six, John Grisham went from being a hardworking, twelve-months-a-year, middle-class sole practitioner in Southaven, Mississippi, to a hardworking, six-months-a-year international celebrity blessed with the Midas touch.

Grisham grew up in modest, tough-love circumstances, with a father who raised cotton and worked construction and a mom who didn't believe in television. By golly, Wanda Grisham's five kids were gonna READ in their spare time. And if they got tired of reading,

then plan B for their evening entertainment was to sit around and listen to family and friends tell stories.

Like all red-blooded American boys of the baby boomer generation, Grisham grew up yearning to be a Major League Baseball player, but that dream ended his sophomore year in college at Delta State University (DSU) in Cleveland, Mississippi. On a fateful day in the fall of 1974, DSU head coach Dave "Boo" Ferriss cut Grisham during baseball tryouts and famously advised the young man, "John, I suggest you forget about baseball and hit the books."

Grisham followed Coach Ferriss's advice. He left DSU, transferred to Mississippi State, majored in accounting, and did well enough to get accepted to Ole Miss Law School. Like most accounting majors who go to law school, Grisham started out wanting to be a tax lawyer. His middle-of-the-pack grade status in his class suggested that, like his baseball dreams, the prospects of his becoming a successful tax attorney at a law firm representing corporate clients was somewhere south of dismal. Again, he got nudged in a new direction by an unlikely source. Ole Miss law professor Robert Khayat taught Grisham torts in the fall of 1978. In his moment of truth taking Khayat's final exam, the young law student was breezing along until he got to the final question. It might as well have been written in Swahili. Grisham turned his imagination loose in writing his "answer," in hopes something he wrote might have some connection to his professor's desired response.

Alas, his final answer proved to be a roundhouse swing and miss, but law professor Khayat saw something in the response that impressed him. When Grisham got back his graded blue book and reviewed his teacher's notations in the margins, next to his answer to the last question, Khayat had written, "You missed all the legal issues but you write great fiction."

After law school graduation in the spring of 1981, Grisham

Facing page: John Grisham. Photo courtesy of Lisa Wadell Buser.

returned to Southaven, Mississippi (where he had gone to high
school), and hung a shingle, open for business to all who walked in
the door. Given the everyman clientele, his practice was made up of
largely criminal and personal injury work. As he told Bill Moyers in
a 2008 PBS interview,

> My clients were working people and poor people—
> victims. People that lost their jobs, that lost their insur-
> ance. But also, on the criminal side, people accused of
> crimes. And that's shaped my life. Because I was always
> fighting for these people against something bigger.[21]

As his clients struggled to pay him, Grisham worked sixty to seventy
hours each week, making his years as a lawyer gritty and anything
but glamorous.

Seeking at least partial relief from his demanding role as Southaven's "lawyer for the little guy," Grisham got elected to serve his
district as a member of the Mississippi House of Representatives
from 1983 to 1990, pulling in a whopping $8,000 per year salary and
reaching the conclusion early on that as far as he was concerned, political office was no place for anyone who aspired to be productive.

Going into 1984, Grisham's assessment of where he was in his
life must have gone something like this: "Okay. Practicing law is an
unprofitable grind. Serving in the legislature looks like it will mainly
involve beating my head against a wall. I've got a wife, two young
kids, and a mortgage. I'm almost thirty years old. Is this all there is?
If not, what else is there?"

Like all ambitious lawyers, John Grisham kept his nose to the
grindstone in his years of practicing law, hoping that somehow,
some way, he could attract a big case to move him to a higher station
in life. In 1984, he got that big case. It just wasn't his case.

That year, a highly publicized trial took place in Southaven at the
DeSoto County Courthouse, involving a criminal defendant indicted
for raping and beating up a young girl. Grisham manipulated his
work schedule to find time to watch the trial. One afternoon after

---

21. "Bill Moyers Talks with John Grisham," January 25, 2008, accessed June 23, 2011, http://www
.pbs.org/moyers/journal/01252008/watch4.html.

most of the evidence had been presented, the judge recessed for a short break, and everyone left the courtroom except two people: John Grisham and the defendant. Grisham, whose daughter was then an infant, looked at the rapist, reflected on everything he'd heard during the trial, and became obsessed with one thought as he stared at the criminal: "If that guy had done to my daughter what he did to the victim in this case, then I would have to kill him."

Though he'd never before written anything in his life except whatever school and practicing law required, John Grisham intuitively knew from his reaction to the rapist in the courtroom that he now had a story he wanted to put into words. He'd watched his wife, Renee, read one mystery after another during their three years of marriage, and he determined that at least some people were making a good living writing novels. Why not give it a try?

He went home from the courthouse, wrote the first chapter, then worked up his courage and asked his wife (the mystery expert) to read it and give him feedback. Renee, not one to pull her punches, held her husband's future writing career in her hands. Would this writing experiment be a short-lived pipe dream, or did Grisham have a secret gift that neither he nor anyone else in the world had ever known about? She read the chapter, then said to her husband the two words he most wanted to hear: "Keep writing."

With Renee's encouragement, Grisham wrote and wrote and wrote over the next three years, producing nine hundred pages (of which over three hundred would later be trashed by an editor). He wrote on a disciplined schedule every morning from 5 to 8:30 a.m. before slogging through his days and nights as a lawyer, legislator, husband, and father. Understandably, battling fatigue became a daily challenge, but the desire to tell the story about "a time to kill," combined with the prospect of doing something that might finally get him into the "major leagues" in at least one arena, kept him on track until he completed the novel.

When Grisham finished, his manuscript got rejected twenty-eight times before Wynwood Press (a minor New York publisher) bought the rights for $15,000 and produced five thousand copies in 1989. Sales of *A Time to Kill* never took off, however, and the lawyer-author sold many of the books out of his car's trunk while making the rounds in small Mississippi towns, speaking at libraries and to civic groups. In the beginning, writing and selling novels seemed every bit as unglamorous and unprofitable as Grisham's legal career, but he didn't give up.

As soon as he finished his first book, and saw a third of it chopped off in the editing process, Grisham decided he'd work a little smarter the second time around. He gained instruction from *Writer's Digest* about a prudent way to outline a novel (which included drafting a two-paragraph summary of what should happen in each chapter, from the beginning of the book to the end, before commencing with writing). Upon completing the outline, he then executed the discipline and created *The Firm*, a book about a young associate at a seemingly successful law firm that operated as an arm of organized crime.

One Sunday morning in 1990, Grisham was at his church in Southaven when Renee called him home immediately. Upon his arrival, she told her husband to phone his agent. Jay Gason advised his client that Paramount had offered $600,000 for the movie rights to *The Firm*, and Doubleday would soon be offering six figures for the book rights. With that kind of payday, within twenty-four hours after the phone call, John Grisham decided his days as a practicing lawyer were over. The rest is history.

Though John Grisham ended his legal career in 1990 due to his overnight success as an author, through his books, he's stayed close to the law—just not as a lawyer. His favorable attitude toward law sharply contrasts with his negative perspective on being a lawyer. While speaking at the Georgetown Law Center in February 2009, Grisham spoke glowingly about the law: "I love the law; I love to study it, I love to read about it, I love to follow it, I love to be frustrated by it."[22]

On his career as a lawyer, he has acknowledged (on the positive side) that his legal training was crucial to his writing legal fiction. But then he admits that the day he closed his law office "was the happiest day of my life; I have not missed it for one moment. It's so much fun to write about lawyers, but I never enjoyed being a lawyer.

---

22. Ann W. Parks, "Georgetown Law Hosts Author John Grisham as Part of Criminal Justice Reform Month," Georgetown Law Web site, accessed September 2, 2011, http://www.law.georgetown.edu/news/webstory/2.26.09.html.

. . . I was so unhappy in that profession I would dream of ways to get out of it."[23] He has further stated that "for lawyers, the main dream of escape is get out of the profession. They dream about a big settlement, a home run, so that they can use the money to do something else."[24]

Despite Grisham's hostile attitude and self-deprecation toward his legal career, in fact he had some success. Early on, he defended a man charged with murder and managed to get him acquitted on grounds of self-defense, despite his client's shooting the victim six times in the head at a range of three inches. On the civil side, he obtained one of the largest settlements in the history of DeSoto County, representing a child severely burned after a water heater exploded. In 1996, six years after his retirement from practicing law, he came back to the courtroom, fulfilling a prior commitment he'd made to the family of a railroad worker killed on the job, and got a $683,500 verdict. Thus, whenever John Grisham produces novels that involve jury trials or the litigation process, he writes with the authenticity of a lawyer who knows the ropes because he's been inside the ropes.

Like Richard North Patterson, as time passed and his fortune went well past financial security, Grisham's writing career evolved beyond creating mere entertaining reads. He explained the transformation in his January 2008 PBS interview with Bill Moyers:

> I write two or three different kinds of books. First, you have the legal thriller, the early books—*The Firm*, *The Pelican Brief*, and *The Client*—that was fresh, it was new, and it was suspenseful, and the books were very popular. And it was just pure entertainment. There was no message. There was no issue. There was nothing serious about the books. . . . And they worked beautifully.
>
> But as the years have gone by, I've caught myself

---

23. " Meet the Writers: John Grisham," accessed May 23, 2011, http://www.barnesandnoble.com/writers/writerdetails.asp?cid=702011.

24. Mel Gussow, "Grisham's Escape into Legal Thrillers," *New York Times*, March 31, 1997, accessed September 12, 2011, http://www.nytimes.com/1997/03/31/books/grisham-s-escape-into-legal-thrillers.html.

more and more taking an issue. When I can take an issue, whether it's the death penalty, or homelessness, or big tobacco, or insurance abuse . . . and wrap a novel around it, and make it compelling, make the pages turn and make it very suspenseful, and get the reader hooked up in the book and also get the reader, for the first time maybe, to think about a problem from a different viewpoint. Those are the best books.[25]

Unlike Richard North Patterson, John Grisham's "issue books" don't present both sides of an issue. What drives his most recent novels is his perception that there are specific, serious wrongs in the legal system that result in egregious social injustice, and he creates a story to dramatize how bad things can get because of those specific wrongs.

His book *The Appeal* (New York: Doubleday, 2008) demonstrates how he develops fiction out of a real life problem that exists in most states today—the partisan political election of trial judges and appellate justices, which can result in a legalized form of bribery. In this novel, Grisham develops a story demonstrating how a successful "little guy" trial plaintiff gets annihilated on appeal by the wealthy defendant who provided the financial support for the election of a new swing-vote justice on the state supreme court.

I addressed the subject of Grisham's power as a novelist-advocate in *The Appeal* in my 2008 column for the *Dallas Business Journal*, reprinted below.[26]

John Grisham and Appellate Politics

John Grisham's new book, *The Appeal*, recently arrived in bookstores. After recent forays into sports fiction, nonfiction, and international espionage, the best-selling

25. "Bill Moyers Talks with John Grisham," January 25, 2008, accessed June 23, 2011, http://www.pbs.org/moyers/journal/01252008/watch4.html.

26. Talmage Boston, "John Grisham and Appellate Politics," *Dallas Business Journal*, February 4, 2008. Reprinted with permission of *Dallas Business Journal*.

author has returned to the genre in which he made his name—the legal thriller.

The Appeal is as much about politics as it is about the legal system, which makes sense given that jurisprudence these days is consumed in politics, whether in the context of the federal courts (where the partisan Senate Judiciary Committee runs roughshod over presidential appointments) or the state courts (where judges in many states, including Texas, are elected in expensive mudslinging political races).

Though the new book is set in Grisham's home state of Mississippi, the scenarios could just as credibly been created in Texas. Ultimately, the question the novel presents is, "Can judicial elections be manipulated by mass quantities of money thrown at defense-oriented (but otherwise unqualified) candidates, whose campaigns are funded and orchestrated by political pros retained by big business—in exchange for the judge's commitment to rule in favor of limited liability in every case, regardless of its particular facts or applicable law?"

That being the question, Grisham's imagination fires on all cylinders in providing the answer. With his customary cynical flair, he serves up some zingers that cut to the heart of today's messed-up judicial/political system that currently serves Texas and other states. Some examples:

• A major chemical company on the wrong side of a $41 million judgment must find a way to get it reversed on appeal. It hires Judicial Vision, a "consulting firm" that explains what it does to its new client, "We do campaigns. We target a Supreme Court justice and take him out." The client responds, "You're saying, for your $8 million fee, I can buy myself a Supreme Court justice who earns $110,000 a year? Politics. I guess that's cheaper than the verdict."
• In the judicial/political campaign, which features a "blitzkrieg" media campaign against the incumbent,

the strategy was simple: "The trick, of course, was to convert Sheila McCarthy from the sensible moderate she was into the raging liberal they needed her to be."

- When Justice Sheila McCarthy is faced with having to write a dissenting opinion in a death penalty case where the defendant was clearly deprived of many constitutional rights, her campaign manager tells her to shelve her dissent until after election day, as she's being hammered by the blitzkrieg for being soft on crime. She acknowledges the obvious, "I'm not a judge anymore. I'm a politician."

- And when the tort reform judicial candidate has his child maimed for life in a clear case of both product liability and medical malpractice, because he's owned by Judicial Vision and its clientele, he knows he must abandon his valid litigation claim. "I can't sue. I'd make a mockery of myself. How can I, a detached jurist, suddenly swap sides because of my family's tragedy?"

Though fictional, these are the sort of tough issues facing today's jurisprudential system. The movement in Texas to have judges appointed on the basis of their qualifications, scholarship, and impartiality is now dormant. Both political parties seem to like having trial judges and appellate justices they can call their own.

In an author's note at the end of the book, Grisham provides a semi-disclaimer that, although his characters and plot are fictional, "there is a lot of truth in this story. As long as private money is allowed in judicial elections, we will see competing interests fight for seats on the bench. The issues are fairly common. Most of the warring factions are adequately described. The tactics are all too familiar. The results are not far off the mark."

Let all the people say "Amen."

As long as Texas requires its judiciary to get elected on the basis of party loyalty and political perspective, then, as John Grisham suggests in *The Appeal*, what makes us think justice and the good guys will prevail in the end?

―――――――――――――――

Though Grisham justifiably prides himself on his vivid imagination, he acknowledged in a 2010 interview that he continues to be inspired by things he remembers from being a lawyer and by actual events, headlines, and current affairs.[27] That statement was certainly true of his inspiration for *The Appeal*. Grisham told Bill Moyers (in his 2008 PBS interview) what was happening to jurisprudence in Mississippi (where the novel is set) and other states that elect judges in partisan political races:

> **John Grisham:** Thirty some odd states elect their judges, which is a bad system. . . . You got corporate people throwing money in. You got big individuals. You got cash coming in to elect a judge who may hear your case. Think about that. You've got a case pending before the court and you want to reshape the structure of the court, well, just get your guy elected. And that's happened in several states. Big money comes in, takes out a bad judge or an unsympathetic judge. Replace him with someone who may be more friendly to you. And he gets to rule in your case without a conflict. . . .
>
> In a state like Mississippi, where the court has now been realigned in such a way where you have a hard right majority. Six or seven. Two or three dissents. When you've got a majority, you only need five. Virtually every plaintiff's verdict is reversed. . . .
>
> So if your neighbor's son gets killed in a car wreck, and there's a big lawsuit, and there's a big verdict against the guilt of the negligent party—or if your friend is injured by a negligent doctor, or a hospital, whatever, you're pretty much out of luck.

―――――――

27. Alysa Goethe, "Author Interview: John Grisham," accessed June 23, 2011. http://www2
.scholastic.com/browse/article.jsp?id=3754317.

Bill Moyers: So the court is now decidedly biased, in your judgment, in favor of the powerful.

John Grisham: Oh, it's not in my judgment. It's a proven fact. You can read the Supreme Court decisions in Mississippi and Alabama; those two states are next door to each other. Both states have a hard right majority. And so people with legitimate claims are, not always, but generally out of luck.

Bill Moyers: Isn't there any outrage among all those good Christian folks, as my mother would say, who live there, who are ordinary folks, little folks?

John Grisham: No. Because they sell it, the Chamber of Commerce sells it. Corporate America sells it and the Republican Party sells it as a way to protect business, economic development, economic growth. "Look at our state. We frown on lawsuits. We frown on unions. This is a good place to do business." That's how you sell it. Sounds good. It's how every politician does it down there. And you end up with a court that's very unsympathetic to the rights of victims, to the rights of consumers, to the rights of criminal defendants. Yeah, that's what happens when those elections, when those types of people are elected.[28]

After *The Appeal* came out in 2008, the precise factual scenario from the book came before the United States Supreme Court in 2009 out of a situation in West Virginia, which the author acknowledged had inspired his novel about appellate politics. A report by the Brennan School of Justice at NYU Law School explained the case of *Caperton v. Massey* (129 S.Ct. 2252 [2009]):

The case, in which coal executive Don Blankenship spent $3 million to help elect Judge Brent Benjamin to the West Virginia Supreme Court in 2004, while his company appealed a $50 million jury award given to a competing coal company, crystallized the threat to due process when seven-figure judicial campaign supporters have business before the courts. When Justice Benjamin cast the tie-breaking vote to overturn the jury award, Hugh Caperton, owner of Harman Mining Corp., said his company's right to a fair and impartial tribunal had been violated.

In the end, the U.S. Supreme Court agreed. Ordering Justice Benjamin to remove himself from the case, the court for the first time ruled that campaign spending could threaten a litigant's due-process rights: "Blankenship's extraordinary contributions were made at a time when he had a vested stake in the outcome," Justice Anthony M. Kennedy wrote for the majority. "Just as no man is allowed to be a judge in his own cause, similar fears of bias can arise when—without the other parties' consent—a man chooses the judge in his own cause."[29]

Did John Grisham's 2008 novel (which sold in the millions), whose facts essentially mirrored *Caperton v. Massey*, have any impact on U.S. Supreme Court swing vote justice Anthony Kennedy, who wrote the 5-4 majority opinion in 2009? Possibly, though we'll never know for sure.

Another controversial issue tackled by the author involving social injustice to the oppressed is the reality that our system of criminal justice sometimes favors finality of result over due diligence in determining whether the right person is on trial and getting convicted for the crime at issue. Grisham delivered his knockout punch to this travesty-of-justice scenario not once but twice—first, in his only nonfiction book, *The Innocent Man* (New York: Doubleday, 2006), and then in fiction with *The Confession* (New York: Doubleday, 2010). My newspaper columns on each book provide the particulars on how our most commercially successful lawyer-novelist maximized his storytelling skills in hopes of preventing future death penalty executions of innocent people:

---

29. James Sample, Adam Skaggs, Jonathan Blitzer, and Linda Casey, *The New Politics of Judicial Elections 2000–2009* (Washington, D.C.: Justice at Stake Campaign, 2010), accessed September 6, 2011. http://brennan.3cdn.net/d091dc911bd67ff73b_09m6yvpgv.pdf.

John Grisham's Blink Experience and
The Innocent Man[30]

Through a fortunate set of circumstances, I became acquainted with John Grisham in 2004. Through an even more fortunate set of circumstances, he agreed to write the foreword to my baseball history book. Late in the year, as I spoke to Mr. Grisham about his foreword, he injected into the conversation the foremost subject on his mind that day.

"Talmage, did you read *The New York Times* obituaries yesterday? Find it. Quick. Read the obit of a guy named Ron Williamson. It's the most dramatic life ever—small town baseball hero heading for professional glory blows out his arm, falls into manic depression and alcoholism, gets convicted of murder and sentenced to death. After spending years on Death Row, his conviction gets reversed because DNA testing proved him innocent. After his release, he finally gets to walk around Yankee Stadium. I think his story is going to be my first non-fiction book."

From that day on, for the next 18 months, John Grisham researched Williamson's life, interviewed those who played roles in it, and wrote *The Innocent Man: Murder and Injustice in a Small Town* (Doubleday 2006), released 3 weeks ago, that now sits at #1 on *The New York Times* non-fiction bestseller list. The author has transformed a 661-word obituary into a 352-page book that may exceed his fiction as a story that holds the reader by the throat until the final chapter ends.

Suffice it to say, the policemen, lawyers, and judges of Ada, Oklahoma, portrayed by Grisham as bumbling, self-righteous buffoons, will not be giving copies of *The Innocent Man* to their friends as Christmas presents this year.

---

30. An earlier version of this article was published in the weekly newspaper *Park Cities People* on November 2, 2006.

The book rakes them over the coals, pours gasoline on their remnants, and then lights up the sky with their debris.

How in the United States of America can such a travesty of justice occur? Easy. Our criminal justice system is and will always be in the hands of fallible people who sometimes believe that getting convictions is their most important responsibility—more important than adhering to the constitutional notion that even an indicted individual is supposed to be presumed innocent until proven guilty.

Though Ron Williamson was a sports hero as a teenager in Ada, when he returned home after his minor league baseball career ended, he morphed into a jerk—a loud, lazy, hard-drinking, skirt-chasing, has-been jock—who local residents grew to loathe. As his mood swings and depression spiraled into full blown mental illness, he changed from being somewhat unappealing into downright despised, and when the murder of a 26-year-old woman went unsolved for 5 years, Ada's law enforcement and jurisprudential sectors decided, against all credible evidence, that Ron should be convicted of the crime, imprisoned, and executed.

Some samples of John Grisham's way with words in telling this amazing story—

- "In rural Oklahoma, virtually all funerals take place with the casket open and positioned just below the pulpit. . . . The reasons for this are unclear and forgotten, but the effect is to add an extra layer of agony to the suffering."
- "Like most crime labs, Oklahoma's was underfunded, understaffed, and under enormous pressure to solve crimes."
- "Nothing makes a small town bar scatter more quickly than a capital murder case. The lawyers flee to their offices, lock their doors, and unplug the phones."
- "When you're on trial for your life, hire either the best

lawyer in town or the worst. Greg had unwittingly hired the worst, and now he had a new trial."

Last year, Malcolm Gladwell had a bestseller titled *Blink: The Power of Thinking Without Thinking* (Little Brown, 2005), a book about making instantaneous decisions based on limited information. As one of his many examples, Gladwell explains, "in the military, brilliant generals are said to possess 'coup d'oeil'—which translated from the French means 'power of the glance': the ability to see and make sense of the battlefield immediately."

John Grisham possesses "coup d'oeil." Responding to a newspaper obituary absorbed in one glance, he has produced a book worthy of the Pulitzer Prize.

The Writer as Entrepreneur and Crusader[31]

Webster's defines entrepreneur as "a person who organizes and manages a business undertaking, assuming the risk for the sake of the profit." As a good entrepreneur, John Grisham writes novels that can be sold in mass quantities—not so he can win literary prizes.

Thus, each of his books is a business undertaking, organized and managed by him. Regarding organization, before Grisham begins writing, he lays out the plot on a page, numbering the lines on the left margin, then drafts a sentence beside each number that provides the essence of what will happen in each chapter of his embryonic novel. Upon completing the outline, he then "manages" to write on a tight timeline, which in recent times has allowed him to produce two books per year.

Other authors have organizational, time management, and writing skills, but what separates John Grisham from the pack is his storytelling imagination.

---

31. Talmage Boston, "The Writer as Entrepreneur and Crusader," *Dallas Business Journal*, December 17, 2010. Reprinted with permission of *Dallas Business Journal*.

Early in his career, Grisham used personal experiences as the inspiration for his novels. After witnessing the trial of a young girl's rapist, and acknowledging that had his daughter been the victim he would have likely murdered the perpetrator, he wrote *A Time to Kill*. The memory of a friend who once returned from an interview with a major law firm, expressing concern about the uneasy undercurrent there, sparked creation of *The Firm*. Using these springboards, Grisham kicked his high-octane mind into overdrive and produced solid fiction.

In his recent books, however, he's been able to use his imagination less. That's because today's legal system—at least in some states—produces more compelling and disturbing stories than any make-believe scenario. When West Virginia allowed a coal company owner who lost a $50 million verdict in a fraud lawsuit to finance a state supreme court candidate's campaign with a $3 million contribution, and get his man elected in time to cast the tie-breaking vote reversing the trial court's judgment, Grisham plugged those facts into his 2008 bestseller, *The Appeal*.

The author's current blockbuster, *The Confession*, released in October, is about Texas and the horrors of our approach to capital punishment. Aided by death row advocate David Dow, Grisham details in his novel how Texas uses the death penalty frequently, efficiently, and erroneously.

Among other things, readers learn the following:

- These days, prosecutors still succeed in eliminating African-Americans as fact finders, allowing all-white juries in trials where black defendants get convicted. Thus, in 2010, a Tom Robinson-type defendant can still get railroaded into a conviction in Texas just like he did in *To Kill a Mockingbird* set in Alabama during the 1930s.
- Semiliterate suspects often unknowingly waive their

right to counsel by signing a paper upon entering the police station, resulting in untaped interrogations, without lawyers, lasting over 10 hours, allowing detectives to use tricks and tell outright lies to manipulate the suspect into a confession.

- In recent years, Texas has had more executions than all other states combined. Our fast track to lethal injection is the quickest in the country.

- A criminal defendant was executed in Texas, and DNA testing later proved that the hair found on the victim was *not* the deceased defendant's hair. As a result, an innocent man had been killed by our state's criminal justice system.

Grisham brings these facts about Texas' criminal justice system to his readers' attention at a time when we are awakening to the death penalty's ugly realities. In November, retired Supreme Court Justice John Paul Stevens explained publicly why he now believes the death penalty is unconstitutional. This month, Houston State District Judge Kevin Fine tried conducting a trial to determine the constitutionality of the Texas death penalty statute.

The author has used perfect timing in bringing out *The Confession* while recognition of capital punishment's moral, factual, and legal deficiencies is heating up. The move is hauntingly reminiscent of what Harper Lee did 50 years ago in getting *To Kill a Mockingbird* published as Martin Luther King began escalating his civil rights movement.

Thus, *The Confession* puts John Grisham in the enviable position of selling millions of books while acting as an authentic crusader against the evils of capital punishment, particularly as administered in Texas.

———————————————

As mentioned in the column, simultaneously with the release of *The Confession* in late 2010, powerful voices across Texas and elsewhere in the country rose in unison to express full-blown out-rage over our criminal justice system and the administration of the death penalty. Surely, they cry out, our legal system must have the goal of achieving justice as its highest priority. Will we get there? If we do, will the impact of Grisham's books be part of what results in a change that reduces the possibility of innocent people getting executed?

Finally, in examining John Grisham's career, recognizing that his "for entertainment only" legal thrillers and his "issue" thrillers have often put lawyers, judges, and our existing system of jurisprudence in an unflattering light—sometimes due to fiction, sometimes due to facts—this profile of him will end on a positive note. In 2010, Grisham (who grew up reading the Hardy Boys and the Chip Hilton mystery series) introduced what he hopes will be a new mystery series aimed at the adolescent market, starting with *Theodore Boone: Kid Law-yer* (New York: Dutton, 2010), followed a year later by *Theodore Boone: The Abduction* (New York: Dutton, 2011). My column on the first book in the series, below, addresses why pursuing this new market appealed to Grisham and what he hopes to accomplish with it.[32]

Summer Reading Kickstart for Kids

School's out. Summer's here. So what are kids going to do the next three months? For those with preteens and young teens, parents' hopes this year match up with where they've been for generations: "Gee, if only little Johnny could discover the joy of pleasure reading . . ."

Yes, imagine if one's child could get motivated to turn off his television and computer, and separate himself from his iPhone so he could devour a book not listed on his school-imposed mandatory summer reading list. Yet what can captivate today's adolescent more than the electronic gadgets at his disposal? Answer: A compelling story.

---

32. An earlier version of this article was published in *Park Cities People* on May 28, 2010.

Reading truth: A great story can only come from a great storyteller, and book-loving adults know that the best storytellers are those writers whose novels fly off stores' shelves and have their pages turned in a blur. Which brings us to John Grisham. Though critics have never compared his prose to Dostoevsky, they've always acknowledged him as a guy who writes tales readers simply can't put down.

Mr. Grisham has now decided he wants to spend part of his time writing stories for children. With the release of his first children's book, *Theo Boone: Kid Lawyer* (Dutton 2010), he's assuming that if grownups manage to be enthralled by his legal thrillers, then their young adolescent offspring ought to connect with a kid-friendly, semi-scaled down version of them. Whereas today's parents once read for pleasure fictional teenaged heroes Nancy Drew, the Hardy Boys, and Chip Hilton, today's pre-adult readers can now have computer-savvy, bicycle-traveling, and compulsively networking eighth grader Theo Boone with whom to engage, as Theo finds himself caught in the middle of his hometown's biggest murder trial ever.

Until now, John Grisham has had a successful career producing fiction (and even one non-fiction book) that paints attorneys and our legal system in a highly unflattering light. Kid lawyer Theo Boone, however, brings a positive spin into the legal mix, as he succeeds in achieving justice when all others involved in the prosecution of defendant Peter Duffy can't quite connect the pertinent dots.

Theo is no ordinary thirteen year old. Growing up as the only child in a house where both parents are practicing lawyers at their own firm and the family practices the ritual of watching and critiquing Perry Mason reruns, when a murder takes place in town, young Mr. Boone seizes the opportunity to put his head into the legal game 24/7. Living in a county seat town means the ever-engaging Theo knows every judge, clerk, and bailiff at the courthouse and spends his free time watching hearings and accessing records on his computer.

This unique environment coupled with Theo's passion to bring about justice produces an eighth grade dynamo who can gather facts, spout law, and counsel his troubled teenaged friends on pet retrieval issues in animal court, child custody issues in family court, foreclosure issues in bankruptcy court, and drug distribution issues in criminal court, as he relentlessly pleases his string of "satisfied clients."

Theo Boone's spunk in the midst of a winding plot should surely captivate young readers this summer, but what will really jerk the hook into kids' mouths is Mr. Grisham's trademark sarcastic sense of humor and his capacity to remember what it was like to be an eighth grader—when tiresome parents repeat the same instructions to their children every day, boys turn inside out in the presence of pretty girls, and daily living is alive with rich possibilities for those like Theo, with the initiative and energy to turn off the electronics and seize the day.

John Grisham recently tested *Theo Boone* on the fifth grade class his daughter teaches, and in his words, the book had an unexpected result. "Several announced that they want to become lawyers."

The good news for parents of young readers is that Mr. Grisham says his new book will be the first in an adventure series he plans to write about Theo Boone with the dual purpose of getting kids into a pleasure reading mode, and also to educate them about the law. As a side benefit, maybe the series will succeed in reducing the summer's consumption of video games and reality TV shows.

Maybe Theo Boone will inspire today's young readers to become lawyers when they grow up, and if he does, maybe they will become the kind of lawyers who John Grisham believes our country will need most in the coming decades, per his remarks to the Ole Miss law students in April 2011 at the ceremony dedicating the new Robert C. Khayat Law Center:

> Perhaps we don't need as many corporate lawyers in tall buildings. Perhaps we don't need as many small town practitioners stacked around the square. Maybe we don't need as many lawyers on government payrolls.
>
> But in this country, and in this state, there is a shortage of lawyers. In this country today, at least half of our people, half of the citizens of this country, do not have access to civil justice.
>
> It's the battered wife who can't hire a lawyer for her divorce or protection. It's the family living in a motel room because the shady bank cut corners on a foreclosure. It's the veteran denied benefits. It's the homeless child denied admission to a local school. It's the migrant worker being paid far less than minimum wage. It's the desperate family of a schizophrenic in need of a facility. It's the honest, hardworking middle-class couple who cannot afford a lawyer to take on their insurance company.
>
> It's a long, sad list, and when you tally it all up, it covers half of us.
>
> Last year the Gates Foundation released the rule of the law report. They looked at all wealthy advanced nations, and their populations' access to civil justice.
>
> The U.S. was dead last.
>
> In Mississippi right now, in Parchman and in the regional prisons, there are hundreds, if not thousands, of innocent people locked up. Victims of a criminal justice system that is broken, they spend their days behind a chain-link fence and razor wire, serving somebody else's time.

They have no lawyers.

There is no one actively on the outside trying to get them out. There is no one fighting the injustice.

I don't speak for this administration, nor do I speak for Robert Khayat. But I hope this law school trains young lawyers who firmly believe that a license to practice law is a powerful tool best used when defending the poor and the weak and the falsely accused.[33]

———

Louis Auchincloss, Richard North Patterson, and John Grisham are leading examples of attorneys and best-selling novelists who have opened the public mind to new perspectives, addressing questions each generation seeks to answer: How do lawyers and judges think? What do clients tell their legal counselors in confidence that sometimes later gets revealed and sometimes remains a secret? Why does drama unfold as it does in courtrooms, where the search for truth and the rules of evidence can conflict? How and why is law affected by politics and vice versa? What happens when our system of justice fails to produce justice?

These are questions with no short, simple, or correct answers, which can sometimes be answered best with stories that entertain, educate, and persuade. Auchincloss, Patterson, and Grisham have all constructed their best-selling novels with foundations built on their time in the trenches as lawyers. If these authors had not brought their legal backgrounds into the books they've written, then their answers to these questions would have been different, and therefore the reading public's answers to these questions would also be different.

33. "Grisham Challenges Law Students to Give Back," *DMonline*, April 17, 2011, http://www.thedmonline.com/article/grisham-challenges-law-students-give-back. Excerpt reprinted with permission of John Grisham.

CHAPTER FOUR

Theodore Roosevelt and the Law: How Leading a Hyperactive Life and Attacking Constitutional Jurisprudence Are Losing Propositions

With the publication in November 2010 of Edmund Morris's final volume in his trilogy of biographies devoted to the life of Theodore Roosevelt, the reading public now has a complete and contemporary assessment of our twenty-sixth president's strengths and weaknesses, demonstrated without ambiguity throughout his many years on center stage. Examining the life of this nonlawyer, who spent much of his life operating in and around the law and performing lawyer-like activities in the company of lawyers, provides delectable food for thought with application to big-picture issues facing attorneys of every generation.

Facing page: Theodore Roosevelt. Photo courtesy of the Library of Congress.

THE SEED OF INSPIRATION

Upon my entry into private practice thirty-three years ago, a partner at my first firm had hanging on his wall the famous "Man in the Arena" excerpt from Roosevelt's speech at the Sorbonne in 1910. I read it then for the first time.

> It is not the critic who counts; not the man who points out how the strong man stumbles or where the doer of deeds could have done them better. The credit belongs to the man who is actually in the arena, whose face is marred by dust and sweat and blood; who strives valiantly; who errs, who comes short again and again, because there is no effort without error and shortcoming; but who does actually strive to do the deeds; who knows great enthusiasms, the great devotions; who spends himself in a worthy cause; who at the best knows in the end the triumph of high achievement, and who at the worst, if he fails, at least fails while daring greatly, so that his place shall never be with those cold and timid souls who neither know victory nor defeat.[1]

The quotation resonated at that formative time on the cusp of my career. It challenged me to make a name in the "arena" of courtrooms, doing what it took to persuade juries, trial judges, and appellate justices of the need to favor my clients' positions. Efforts in the legal arena on my horizon would surely require "striving valiantly" with "great enthusiasms" and "great devotion," so as to fully "spend myself for a worthy cause."

This focused goal of becoming a litigator who fulfilled Roosevelt's "man in the arena" ideal became blurred in the fourth year of my career. My legal mentor at the time, Walter Spradley, offered me the chance to leave the firm where we (until then) had worked together and go off with him, which would require changing my practice from being a courtroom lawyer to a transactional lawyer. Upon telling Walter my preference was to stay where I was and stick

---

1. Theodore Roosevelt, "The Man in the Arena: Citizenship in a Republic," Paris, France, April 23, 1910, accessed August 18, 2011, www.theodoreroosevelt.org/research/speech%20arena.htm.

with litigation, he said, "I understand your decision, but let me tell you something. My experience in watching lawyers over the last forty years is that litigators are like pilots. I know a lot of old pilots, and I know a lot of bold pilots, but I don't know a lot of old, bold pilots."

Since that conversation with Walter Spradley, my time in the litigation arena has lasted three decades and hopefully will continue into the future. Having seen scores of good lawyers flame out (like bold pilots) over the years for a multitude of reasons, it recently occurred to me that fully exploring Roosevelt, the source of my career aspiration as a young lawyer, would be a worthwhile exercise for purposes of exploring how his performing nonstop for decades at the highest level had affected him over the course of his life.[2] At the outset of my research, I knew of his death at age sixty, which proved Walter's point that Roosevelt had not lived to be an "old, bold pilot."

ROOSEVELT THE HUMAN PHENOMENON

Over the course of his trilogy on Theodore Roosevelt, Edmund Morris quotes dozens of Roosevelt's peers in their description of his personality and energy level, which dominated every arena Roosevelt entered over the course of his life. Those who encountered him frequently commented on his abounding vitality, and his inhu-

---

2. Although there are dozens of outstanding Roosevelt biographies, my research focused on the work of three authors. As my primary sources, I reviewed the books of Edmund Morris, who won the Pulitzer Prize for *The Rise of Theodore Roosevelt* (New York: Coward, McCann, & Geoghegan, 1979) about Roosevelt's life from birth until he became president in 1901. This book was followed by the critically acclaimed *Theodore Rex* (New York: Random House, 2001) about Roosevelt's White House years. Morris concluded his series with *Colonel Roosevelt* (New York: Random House, 2010) about the decade of Roosevelt's post-presidential years until his death in 1919. My secondary source was the concise biography *Theodore Roosevelt* (New York: Henry Holt & Company, 2001), written by esteemed writer and lawyer Louis Auchincloss. Auchincloss's examination of Roosevelt's life through the eyes of an attorney confirmed how Roosevelt's life story provides insight for those practicing in today's legal profession. My final source was *The Wilderness Warrior: Theodore Roosevelt and the Crusade for America* (New York: HarperCollins, 2009) by Douglas Brinkley, professor of history at Rice University and a contributing editor at *Vanity Fair* magazine. Although Mr. Brinkley's book ends with Roosevelt leaving the presidency in 1909, it opens the door to a clearer understanding of what made Roosevelt tick, as Brinkley relies on the persuasive psychiatric assessment of Roosevelt made by Johns Hopkins Medical School professor of psychiatry Kay Redfield Jamison.

man energy reminded many of a high-speed locomotive. Douglas Brinkley, likewise, in his book, provided depictions of Roosevelt's vivacious personality as described by the president's compatriots. Brinkley noted that journalist William Allen White articulated the clearest depiction of Roosevelt as a unique force of nature: "There was no twilight and evening star for him. He plunged headlong snorting into the breakers of the tide that swept him to another bourne, full armed breasting the waves, a strong swimmer undaunted."[3]

Such similar reactions result from Roosevelt's never having had a sense of moderation in any activity he pursued. Morris provides the necessary supporting details over the course of his trilogy to establish the proposition that everything Roosevelt did, he did ferociously. When he wrote, he wrote at a frenetic pace—whipping out twenty-five letters in a morning and writing 83,000 words in three weeks while creating one of his books. When working on his cattle ranch in the Dakota Territory, Roosevelt earned the respect of his fellow cowboys as someone who could ride a hundred miles in a day, stay up all night on watch, and then be ready again for work after an early breakfast. When he campaigned for the presidency, he delivered thirty speeches in a day from his train at whistle stops and got his energy level up for them by shadowboxing in the caboose. In recreational exercise at tennis, he played ninety-one games in one day and would celebrate his good shots by shrieking, laughing, and hopping around on one foot. With those kinds of activities happening routinely, consistent adjectives and metaphors repeatedly flowed from amazed observers.

ROOSEVELT AND THE LAW

The previously cited words and deeds encapsulate the essence of Roosevelt's personality and his over-the-top pursuit of life in many arenas and lay the predicate for making the connection between Roosevelt, on one hand, and law and lawyers, on the other. Though not a lawyer, Roosevelt spent his adult life pushing the

3. Brinkley, *The Wilderness Warrior*, 12.

envelope of hyperactivity at all times in the following "arenas" in the midst of law, lawyers, and legal situations:

Law student. After graduating from Harvard College, he attended Columbia Law School, where he became conspicuous for frequently interrupting classes by firing questions at his professors. He soon concluded that lawyers and judges preferred legalese to his notions of "justice," and he quit law school after one year. In particular, Roosevelt the law student was deeply offended by the doctrine of caveat emptor ("let the buyer beware"). Morris concluded that Roosevelt lost interest in law school because he was "impatient with logic," intolerant of corporation lawyers' "sharp practices," and had no interest in what he perceived to be the law's arcane "intricacies."[4]

Lawmaker. Since he had planned to use his legal studies solely as a stepping stone to politics, upon quitting Columbia he got himself elected as a New York State assemblyman at age twenty-three, where he immediately became involved in the business of creating and debating legislation, much of it aimed at uncovering and eliminating the problematic connections between businessmen and politicians. To get recognized on the state house floor, the young 5'8" legislator would often jump up and stand on his chair, calling out "Mister Speaker, Mister Speaker!"

Prosecutor. Following his three terms in the legislature, he became a civil service commissioner in Washington, DC (1889–1895), then a New York City police commissioner (1895–1896). In both positions, he acted as an investigator, enforcer of laws, and prosecutor of corrupt public officials. Unburdened by judges or evidentiary rules, he became famous for his energetic cross-examinations of wrongdoers, in which he was so forceful that he often interrupted his targets with new questions before they could complete their answers. Morris recounts Roosevelt's self-righteous attitude in this line of work, as he remembered it fondly later in life: he would claim that justice was justice "because I did it."[5]

---

4. Morris, *The Rise of Theodore Roosevelt*, 118, 119.

5. Ibid., 430.

Conflict strategist. At age thirty-eight, Roosevelt became assistant secretary of the United States Navy and immediately began running the Navy and increasing the number of American warships, while his superior alternately suffered illness and enjoyed long vacations. Roosevelt avoided international altercations for the first twelve months on the job despite his aggressive posturing, until engineering the start of the Spanish-American War. In every transaction involving potential conflict, Roosevelt adhered to his famous slogan that guided all his diplomatic strategies: "Speak softly and carry a big stick."

Combatant. He left his executive position with the Navy in early 1898 to fulfill his greatest ambition—to fight in a war—training and then leading his famed Rough Riders on their charge up San Juan Hill, the tipping point in the United States' liberation of Cuba from the Spaniards. This brief successful taste of battle on July 1, 1898, never left Roosevelt's mouth for the rest of his life. In fact, thereafter, he often referred to his time at San Juan Hill as the greatest day of his life, and the experience undoubtedly exacerbated his natural pugnacity in all future dealings.

Client. Returning from Cuba a national hero, Roosevelt ran for governor of New York in 1898. Since residency in the state was required of gubernatorial candidates, his campaign nearly imploded over his having sworn on his most recent tax return that he (in his last prewar position as assistant secretary of the Navy) was a resident of Washington, DC. Roosevelt retained stalwart Wall Street lawyer Elihu Root to do what was necessary to make him an eligible candidate. Using the law's "intricacies," Root's "sharp practice" in finding a favorable interpretation of the word *resident* won the day. With that obstacle cleared, Roosevelt was elected and served two years as New York's head of state before his selection as President William McKinley's running mate in 1900.

Litigation instigator and hardball mediator. After McKinley's assassination six months into his second term in September 1901, Roosevelt became president, thereby achieving at the youngest age in American history what he believed to be the highest form of success that a motivated person could achieve. In his seven and a half years in the Oval Office, the United States for the most part prospered and stayed out of war.

On the national front, realizing (from his successful dealings with Elihu Root) the value of skilled lawyers when confronting highly complicated legal issues, he relied on Philander Knox as attorney general. He directed Knox to bust trusts and destroy monopolies, which Knox successfully accomplished, most notably in the *Northern Securities* case[6] that went the federal government's way all the way through the Supreme Court.

When a coal workers' strike in the winter of 1902 threatened to freeze many American people to death, Roosevelt jumped into the "arena" and threatened to use the "big stick" of military intervention to take over the mines. The strong-armed mediation tactic worked and caused the owners and miners to capitulate and agree to settle their dispute through binding arbitration.

His talents in resolving disputes were then extended into the international realm as he used the "big stick" of the U.S. Navy's sizable firepower in 1902 to intimidate Germany into backing off from its effort to bombard Venezuela after the South American country had defaulted on a sizeable debt. In 1903, Roosevelt provided necessary resources to enable Panama's gaining independence from Colombia, again avoiding war, which allowed for the construction of the Panama Canal and the United States' gaining control over the Canal Zone.

Such successes in resolving international conflicts caused the leaders of Russia and Japan to select President Roosevelt as their mediator, charged with the task of bringing an end to the Russo-Japanese War. After months of shrewd negotiations, Roosevelt succeeded in delivering peace to Northeast Asia in August 1905. Roosevelt delighted in being center stage in big-time mediation because, as with his duties as civil service commissioner and New York police commissioner, there were no rules, restrictions, lawyers, or judges to inhibit his actions, which were aimed at achieving his goal of final resolution.

---

6. *Northern Securities Co. v. United States*, 193 U.S. 197 (1904).

Auchincloss recognized Roosevelt's preference for operating in a mode disconnected from law and lawyers by providing Supreme Court Justice Oliver Wendell Holmes's response to criticism leveled at him by President Roosevelt after Holmes had dissented in the *Northern Securities* opinion. When Roosevelt claimed that he could "carve a better judge out of a banana," Holmes indicated that the insult didn't bother him; he agreed with an unnamed senator's quip about the president: "What the boys like about Roosevelt is that he doesn't give a damn about the law."[7]

Before leaving the White House, Roosevelt received a rare comeuppance from the law. After Joseph Pulitzer's newspaper criticized him for making misrepresentations about his policy in Panama, Roosevelt directed Attorney General Knox to sue Pulitzer for criminal libel. The defendant prevailed easily, and Auchincloss regarded Roosevelt's decision to pursue the unwinnable case as a bona fide "foolish act."

Party to lawsuits. Being defeated by Pulitzer did not stop Roosevelt from being involved in litigation after his departure from the Oval Office. In the ten years of Roosevelt's life after leaving the White House, he was a party to two libel cases, first as a plaintiff and then as a defendant, both of which resulted in highly publicized jury trials and both of which he won, the courtroom becoming an outlet to satisfy Roosevelt's proclivity for combat.

The first trial took place in May 1913 in Marquette, Michigan. George Newett, publisher of a nearby small-town newspaper and a lifelong Republican, felt betrayed when Roosevelt left the party in 1912 to run for president on the Bull Moose ticket, opposing the incumbent Republican, President William Howard Taft (in advance of the election ultimately won by Woodrow Wilson). Newett took out his anger over Roosevelt's departure from and damage to the GOP by writing a scathing editorial in which he claimed Roosevelt "lies and curses in a most disgusting way; he gets drunk too, and all his intimates know it."[8]

---

7. Auchincloss, *Theodore Roosevelt*, 53.

8. Morris, *Colonel Roosevelt*, 243.

Yes, the former president had a red face (caused by high blood pressure), and yes, he often became so animated he gave the appearance of being intoxicated (though, in fact, he was merely "drunk" on living an exuberant life), but no witness could be found to support Newett's allegation that Roosevelt had ever imbibed alcohol in excess. Roosevelt testified himself about his very moderate intake of alcohol over the course of his life and produced an army of corroborating doctors and VIP witnesses. Finally, Newett took the witness stand and acknowledged that his statements had been based on unsubstantiated hearsay, that he had no witnesses to support his claims, and that he had written the editorial solely for political reasons.

With his reputation repaired by Newett's testimony, Roosevelt backed off from seeking actual and punitive damages and asked the court to instruct the jury that he desired only nominal damages. For his countless hours spent (over the course of eight months) in the preparation and trial of the case, and having incurred sizeable legal fees and travel expenses for his witnesses, Roosevelt ended up with a cleared name—and a favorable verdict of six cents.

Two years later, in 1915, Roosevelt came to trial as a defendant, after being sued for libel by New York Republican Party leader William Barnes, who sought $50,000 in damages (big money in those days). The case arose from Roosevelt's public statement in 1914 that Barnes was part of New York's "alliance between crooked business and crooked politics."[9] He went to trial in Syracuse, having to prove the truth of his accusation against Barnes. After a five-week trial, the jury deliberated almost two days before finding in favor of the former president. Morris vividly details the trial for twenty pages in *Colonel Roosevelt* and establishes that although Roosevelt's position was less than air tight, his courtroom presence and personality held the jury spellbound, allowing him to prevail because he was "a defendant beyond the reach of ordinary justice."[10]

---

9. Ibid., 366.

10. Ibid., 424.

In the context of his extended connections with law, lawyers, lawsuits, and engaging in lawyer-like activities, Roosevelt had a life-long perception (which became amplified as time went on) that whatever he believed to be the best and most efficient course of action for dealing with a particular political situation should undoubtedly become the ultimate course of action taken by everyone else. Moreover, on taking a position, he seemed unable or unwilling to later question whether it was, in fact, the correct one. For instance, while president, he dishonorably discharged 167 African American soldiers over their alleged participation in a Texas riot, based on very sketchy evidence. After being criticized for his decision, Roosevelt expressed that he felt "profound indifference" to any attacks leveled against him regarding the matter.

In his post-presidency years, whenever his headstrong political positions came in conflict with existing law, Roosevelt pursued an ill-conceived strategy to deal with that circumstance. In 1910, following a ten-month safari in Africa and a heady tour of Europe, during which he was treated with great pomp and circumstance as the most esteemed and popular leader in the world, Roosevelt returned to the United States and began advocating what he called the "New Nationalism," which had as its primary objective eliminating big business's control over politics. Accomplishing such a goal would require massive federal regulation, which would necessarily conflict with (1) existing statutes and (2) corporations' common law property rights. What to do about that conflict? For Roosevelt, the answer was simple: repeal the statutes and change the common law of property to favor the rights of individuals over the rights of corporations.

At a speech to thirty thousand people in Kansas on August 31, 1910, he proclaimed that "if we do not have the right kind of law and the right kind of administration of the law, we cannot go forward as a nation. . . . [O]ur public men [i.e., legislators and judges] must be genuinely progressive."[11] In one paragraph, Morris succinctly addresses Roosevelt's direct challenge to the American legal system at the outset of the twentieth century's second decade:

---

11. Theodore Roosevelt, "The New Nationalism," Osawatomie, Kansas, August 31, 1910, accessed August 18, 2011, http://theodore-roosevelt.com/images/research/speeches/trnationalismspeech.pdf.

In no way did Roosevelt seem more radically threatening than in his moralistic attitude toward justice. If constructionists could believe their ears and eyes, he proposed to subject the Constitution itself to moral review. "When I see you," [long-time friend] Henry Cabot Lodge wrote on 5 September, "I shall want to have a full talk in regard to this matter of court decisions, about which I admit I am very conservative. . . . The courts are charged with the duty of saying what the law is, not what it ought to be, and I think to encourage resistance to the decisions of the courts tends to lead to a disregard of the law."[12]

Roosevelt followed the Kansas speech with others, all highly critical of the existing framework of law, which he believed to be biased in favor of big business. In *Colonel Roosevelt*, Morris points out that Roosevelt's perspective in 1910 flowed naturally from his lifetime attitude toward law:

Shadows over substance, words rather than deeds, precedents hampering change, technical injustice precluding practical justice: Roosevelt had been attacking statutory pedantry since his days as a law student at Columbia University. . . . As President, he insisted that courts, no less than churches, were places where plain morals had to be expounded. Judges should no more sanction an abusive policy, in the name of the Fourteenth Amendment, than priests should cite the Old Testament in favor of child sacrifice. He had gone so far as to suggest, in his eighth [and final] annual message to Congress, that the judicial branch of government was actually a branchlet of the legislative.[13]

Despite criticism of his radical attitude toward the law by his close friends (and highly esteemed lawyers) Henry Cabot Lodge and Elihu Root, Roosevelt continued on with his crusade against American jurisprudence to the point that by 1912, he wrote an article for

12. Morris, *Colonel Roosevelt*, 111.

13. Ibid., 119.

The Outlook magazine calling for political referendums across the country to have judicial decisions recalled and removed as precedent. Morris says the article caused Republican leaders to wonder, knowing that Roosevelt was contemplating running for president again, "What socialist mayhem would he visit upon the courts, if by some perversion of democracy he returned to the White House?"[14]

His desire to put into place legislation that would empower American voters to repeal what Roosevelt perceived as erroneous judicial decisions expanded to the point that he began advocating the next step in his full-throttle attack on the American legal system—urging that voters be given the right to vote federal and state judges off the bench, including United States Supreme Court justices, upon their issuing opinions out of step with Roosevelt's progressive political agenda. Roosevelt expounded on his anti-independent judiciary philosophy in a speech to the Ohio constitutional convention in early 1912:

> I do not believe in adopting the recall save as a last resort. . . . But either the recall will have to be adopted or else it will have to be made much easier than it now is to get rid, not merely of a bad judge, but of a judge who, however virtuous, has grown so out of touch with social needs and facts that he is unfit longer to render good service on the bench. . . .
>
> When a judge decides a Constitutional question, when he decides what the people as a whole can and cannot do, the people should have the right to recall that decision if they think it wrong. We should hold the judiciary in all respect, but it is both absurd and degrading to make a fetish of a judge or of any one else.[15]

When President Taft (a constitutional law scholar who had served as Roosevelt's secretary of war for four years and would later become chief justice of the United States Supreme Court after leav-

---

14. Ibid., 161.

15. Theodore Roosevelt, "A Charter of Democracy," Columbus, Ohio, February 21, 1912, accessed August 18, 2011, http://theodore-roosevelt.com/images/research/txtspeeches/704.pdf.

ing the White House) learned of the speech in Ohio, and aware of his predecessor's transparent desire to return to the Oval Office, he pulled no punches in responding to Roosevelt's preposterous position, at a speech in Boston:

> One who so lightly regards constitutional principles, and especially the independence of the judiciary, one who is naturally so impatient of legal restraints, and of due legal procedure, and who has so misunderstood what liberty regulated by law is, could not be safely entrusted with successive [*sic*] presidential terms. I say this sorrowfully, but I say it with the full conviction of truth.[16]

Morris reports that after finishing his speech, President Taft was so despondent over having to engage in such an antagonistic confrontation with the man he had admired so long and so deeply, who had now twisted off into such irrationality as to advocate rejecting the American system of dispensing justice, that when he got on the train to his next destination, he "put his head in his hands and cried."[17]

Auchincloss determined that it was at this point in 1912, when Roosevelt first began advocating the outrageous position he called "Initiative, Referendum and Recall," that the change in Roosevelt following his triumphant tour of Europe (in 1910) was recognizable not as change for the better but as a change for evil. Roosevelt increasingly became vindictive and completely intolerant of any opposition.

At this critical turning point, when Roosevelt decided his political perspective was so essential to advancing American society that his leading the country became a priority over the constitutional commitment to an independent judiciary and the rule of law, he "threw his hat in the ring" and challenged the incumbent, William Howard Taft, for the Republican presidential nomination in 1912.

Fortunately, Roosevelt's effort to unseat Taft went down in flames at the National Republican convention in Chicago, but only after giving a last ditch appeal to the delegates. In the final sentence

---

16. Morris, *Colonel Roosevelt*, 185.

17. Ibid.

of his convention speech, Roosevelt asserted his belief that he had been called to regain the White House as God's political agent, telling the crowd, "We fight in honorable fashion for the good of mankind; fearless of the future; unheeding of our individual fates; with unflinching hearts and undimmed eyes; we stand at Armageddon, and we battle for the Lord."[18] Morris notes that after delivering this "evangelical" speech, a flyer mocking Roosevelt circulated throughout Chicago claiming that, "At three o'clock, Thursday afternoon, Theodore Roosevelt will walk on the waters of Lake Michigan."[19]

After Roosevelt lost his bid for the Republican presidential nomination, his disciples instantly formed the Progressive "Bull Moose" Party with Roosevelt's blessing, and they held their own convention in Chicago seven weeks after the Republicans left town. There they kept the religious fervor flowing—singing together "Onward Christian Soldiers" as Roosevelt delivered his acceptance speech, entitled "A Confession of Faith," which ended with the exact line he had used to close his Republican convention speech: "We stand at Armageddon and we battle for the Lord." Incredibly, Roosevelt actually believed he was on a mission from God to regain the White House regardless of which political party he represented.

Ironically (and perhaps hypocritically), while Roosevelt drove his political supporters into a religious fervor and encouraged them to believe he and God were politically aligned in the 1912 presidential campaign, in point of fact, Theodore Roosevelt was not a deeply religious person. Throughout his life, though he attended Protestant churches, he expressed doubts about the existence of heaven and an afterlife. While president, he sought to remove the words "In God We Trust" from the face of coins. Brinkley makes clear that the most inspirational book of Roosevelt's life was Darwin's *The Origin of Species,* not the Bible. Morris provides this description of Roosevelt's faith:

18. Theodore Roosevelt, "Case Against the Reactionaries," Chicago, Illinois, June 17, 1912, accessed August 18, 2011, http://theodore-roosevelt.com/images/research/speeches/trreactionaires.pdf.

19. Morris, *Colonel Roosevelt*, 198.

To him, no faith was superior to another, and none to the dignity of individual will. . . . He had no capacity for devotion, unless his love of nature qualified as that. . . . Aside from a few clichés of Protestant rhetoric, the gospel he preached had always been political and pragmatic. He was inspired less by the Passion of Christ than by the Golden Rule.[20]

Something obviously happened to Roosevelt in his post-presidential decade of life that caused him to lose his bearings and enter a heightened state of disequilibrium, increasingly seeing himself as the messianic messenger of the Bull Moose Party's semireligious movement and as a person at war with law, lawyers, the rule of law, and the American legal system.

His longtime friend and legal adviser, Elihu Root, who had served with distinction in Roosevelt's cabinet during Roosevelt's first term, joined President Taft in mourning his former boss's loss of emotional and intellectual balance. Root sent a letter to Roosevelt's Harvard classmate Robert Bacon (who had served briefly as Roosevelt's secretary of state), indicating his extreme grief over the former president's demise into the dark side, particularly as he and many of his colleagues now found themselves unable to go along with Roosevelt.

As Roosevelt left his lawyer and other friendships behind, and commenced his campaign as the Bull Moose presidential candidate, his speeches attacking the effectiveness of the American legal system became more radical. Roosevelt advised the public that earlier attempts to control the power of large corporations by means of antitrust lawsuits had been unsuccessful, and "the effort at prohibiting all combination has substantially failed. The way out lies, not in attempting to prevent such combinations, but in completely controlling them in the interest of the public welfare."[21] In other words, he was asking the American people to elect him as their president and let him control the federal government, its legal system, and its

---

20. Ibid., 35–36.

21. "The New Nationalism," Osawatomie, Kansas, August 31, 1910, accessed August 18, 2011, http://theodore-roosevelt.com/images/research/speeches/trnationalismspeech.pdf.

large corporations, on the premise that his unilateral executive action would make the country better and he would single-handedly strip big business of its power.

ROOSEVELT'S UNHAPPY ENDING

Roosevelt's post-presidency downward spiral manifested itself in a myriad of disturbing ways. Morris and other sources describe the following examples of Roosevelt as a man who lost control of himself in his final years:

- He stuffed himself three times a day with huge meals (breakfast alone usually consisted of eating twelve fried eggs and drinking a gallon of coffee) and gained considerable weight.

- After being shot in the chest by an assassin in October 1912 while campaigning for president as the Bull Moose nominee, he insisted on giving a speech (lasting eighty minutes) while blood flowed through his shirt and the right side of his body turned black. Morris riffs on Roosevelt's bizarre reaction to being shot, to the effect that Roosevelt's conduct in the immediate aftermath of the assassination attempt, one month before election day, was a statement to the voting public of the sincerity of his religious political movement: "This is my body, this is my blood. The mock-religious aura that had glowed around Roosevelt since he first stood at Armageddon had reached its grotesque climax."[22]

- Overweight and out of shape, Roosevelt took an extended trip to South America in 1914, where he nonchalantly confronted piranhas, anacondas, blood-sucking bats, and bloodthirsty pium flies, before contracting malaria, from which he never fully recovered.

---

22. Morris, *Colonel Roosevelt*, 247.

- He repeatedly and publicly called President Woodrow Wilson a "coward" for his delay in injecting American military forces into the battlefront of World War I.

- When Wilson finally committed the United States to the war, though Roosevelt was sickly, tired, and old beyond his years at age fifty-eight, he repeatedly begged the president to allow him to organize a new regiment of Rough Riders to engage in battle on the European front.

- When Wilson refused Roosevelt's offer to fight, Roosevelt pulled all his political and military strings to get all four of his sons onto the front lines of battle—where two were soon seriously wounded and his youngest son, Quentin, was killed. Auchincloss wrote that, in particular, Roosevelt's efforts as an ill and elderly man to get to the trenches and to have his sons rushed to the front lines of battle in Word War I demonstrated the former president's severe cognitive decline.

- On the day he learned of Quentin's death, after hearing the tragic news, Roosevelt insisted on fulfilling a commitment to give a speech to the New York State Republican Convention.

On Christmas Eve of 1918, knowing his days were numbered, he told his sister Corinne that he had "kept the promise that I made to myself when I was twenty-one. . . . I promised myself that I would work *up to the hilt* until I was sixty, and I have done it."[23] Thirteen days later, Roosevelt died, and his death certificate stated the cause of his death was "an embolism of the lung, with multiple arthritis as a contributory factor," though Morris offers evidence that what really killed him may have been a broken heart caused by six months of deep grieving over the death of his youngest son.

LIFE LESSONS FOR LAWYERS

Therefore, what? Exactly what lessons are there for lawyers to learn from the life of Theodore Roosevelt?

---

23. Morris, *Colonel Roosevelt*, 549.

First, although a highly electric life, "in the arena," can produce achievements, drama, and exhilaration, it can also become so
intoxicating as to cause someone to lose his bearings because of
ill-considered notions of infallibility, and it can further become so
exhausting as to cause that same someone to self-destruct mentally,
physically, morally, and prematurely. It is why bold pilots don't live
to be old pilots.

Yes, Roosevelt had a remarkable life, center stage, "in the arena,"
whenever he could get there—an East Coast scholar, a cowboy of
the Wild West, an acclaimed naturalist, a war hero, the youngest
president in American history, the creator of the Panama Canal,
the supreme mediator who ended the Russo-Japanese War, the trust
buster who put teeth into our antitrust laws, the resurrector and
defender of the Monroe Doctrine (to keep European control out
of the Western Hemisphere), the expander of America's national
park and wildlife refuge system, and the author of more than twenty
books, many of which were critically acclaimed. Arguably, in his
White House years, Roosevelt achieved more good things for the
country than any other American president, and his performance in
the Oval Office is always rated by historians in their many polls to
be among the five greatest in history.

And yet . . . and yet . . . after leaving the Oval Office, the glory
and popularity he had earned both nationally and internationally
went to his head. His outrageously egotistical comment upon leaving the White House became a self-fulfilling prophecy: "No man in
American public life has ever reached the crest of the wave as I appear to have done without the wave's breaking and engulfing him."[24]
With each successive year following his presidency, he became more
and more out of control, and in that mode, inevitably the waves
broke and engulfed him.

In his biography, Brinkley endorsed Dr. Kay Jamison's psychiatric assessment of Roosevelt, which appeared in her book *Exuber-
ance: The Passion for Life* (New York: Alfred A. Knopf, 2004). Dr.
Jamison presents Roosevelt as the poster child for both the bright
and the dark sides of an exuberant personality, and her description

---

24. Ibid., 33.

of the exuberant manic state squares up on all fours with the life and personality of Theodore Roosevelt.

According to Dr. Jamison, people with manic-depressive illness are more likely to be impulsive, to be utterly certain of their convictions, and to be susceptible to dangerous rushes of adrenaline, when manic. Further, although manic thought may initially travel in a straight line, it devolves into chaos as the mania progresses.

Rapid talking, marked by intentionally clicking the teeth, biting off syllables with fervor, pounding the fist while making points, and a capacity to absolutely dominate (and yes, hog) conversations are all characteristics of the manic personality (as Morris demonstrates throughout his trilogy on Roosevelt), and all were characteristic of Roosevelt's verbal communications throughout his adult life.

In *The Wilderness Warrior*, Brinkley does a superb job of summarizing Dr. Jamison's findings on the exuberant manic depression mind-set as applied to Roosevelt's personality and how it led to his post-presidency demise:

> Roosevelt is exhibit A for this condition. His set of symptoms—propulsive behavior, deep grief, chronic insomnia, and an all-around hyperactive disposition— demonstrate both the manic and the depressive phases of bipolar disorder. Too often, Dr. Jamison argued, people mistakenly thought manic depression meant despondence and withdrawal from human endeavors. Usually it does. But those afflicted with exuberance, she argued, go in the opposite direction; behaving as relentless human blow-torches they're unable to turn down their own flame. Diagnosing Roosevelt's medical condition more than eighty years after his death, Jamison claimed that the highs of the exuberance phase brought many wonderful gifts; but, she warned, there was also a sharp-edged downside. Living by throwing up skyrockets—as P.T. Barnum once put it—wore one down to nothing. No sleep, for example, wasn't good for the heart or other vital organs. Only by exhausting oneself in physical activity—like climbing Mount Katahdin or ice skating on the Charles River in a

winter storm—could an exuberant manic like Roosevelt turn himself off.[25]

Early in *The Rise of Theodore Roosevelt*, Morris provides a prophetic quote from novelist Henry James, in which James refers to Roosevelt as "a wonderful little machine" that performs astonishingly but is likely destined to be overstrained. Morris later continues the prophecy in *Theodore Rex* with the same metaphor offered more than a decade later during Roosevelt's White House years. Irving Fisher, a fitness and nutritional expert of the era, claimed: "It is clear to me that the President is running his machine too hard. . . . In another decade or two . . . I would almost risk my reputation as a prophet in predicting that he will find friction in the machine, which will probably increase to almost the stopping point."[26]

In providing a lesson for all who aspire to spend maximum time "in the arena," the life of Theodore Roosevelt can be compared to the finest Mercedes-Benz being steered by a mad scientist obsessed with keeping his gas pedal floored at all times, as the manic driver exhilarates in his own amazing achievement at navigating the dizzying high speed ride . . . for a while. But then, his vehicle begins showing telltale signs of malfunction from being misused and abused, until it finally collapses in a heap long before its warranty period ends.

The second lesson to retain from Roosevelt's life is that any person, no matter how spectacular his career achievements, no matter how dynamic his personality may be, who loses respect for the constitutional imperative of an independent judiciary, guided by the rule of law to preside over society's disputes, has officially lost his moral compass; and it is incumbent that that person's errant voice be silenced by lawyers, judges, and all others committed to protecting our American legal system.

Roosevelt's disrespect for the law began with his dropping out of Columbia Law School. As federal civil service commissioner,

25. Brinkley, *The Wilderness Warrior*, 123–124.

26. Morris, *Theodore Rex*, 452.

then New York police commissioner, and finally while president acting as national and international mediator—in all these quasi-legal positions, where he called the shots essentially without legal restrictions—Roosevelt operated from the vainglorious perspective that in his perfect world, justice was justice "because I did it."

Brinkley brings out a corollary to Roosevelt's joy in creating justice outside of courtrooms when he describes Roosevelt's capacity to create legislation, instantly, to protect wildlife refuges during his presidency:

> [In a meeting with his advisers] Roosevelt asked, "Is there any law that will prevent me from declaring Pelican Island a Federal Bird Reservation?" The answer was a decided "No," the island, after all, *was* federal property. "Very well then," Roosevelt said with marvelous quickness. "I So Declare It."[27]

As president, when operating outside the mediation and wilderness refuge arenas, Roosevelt often found himself in unpleasant circumstances, where laws, rules, and statutes were binding upon him, and lawyers and judges were in place to make sure he obeyed them, regardless of how much he personally "didn't give a damn about the law." Naturally, he favored a dependent judiciary who saw "justice" being served for the highest good when administered in accordance with his personal vision. Auchincloss pointed out that Roosevelt expected any judge he appointed to do his best to carry out the spirit of the law as interpreted by the party in power, and his idea of a great constitutional lawyer was one who would always agree with him.

Thus, like most presidents, during his White House years, Roosevelt wanted federal courts to rule and the Constitution to be interpreted one way—his way. However, with an attitude unlike most presidents, when judges saw issues differently than he did, Roosevelt believed they were purposefully betraying his trust. Small wonder that after leaving the White House, as judgments and appellate opinions got rendered by various courts at odds with his desires,

---

27. Brinkley, *The Wilderness Warrior*, 14.

Roosevelt attempted to persuade the American electorate to vote for the repeal of those errant decisions and for the immediate removal from the bench of those errant judges who had authored those opinions. Fortunately, his crazed pitch for personal power over the rule of law was rejected by the American people, who took their cues from the leading constitutional lawyers and judges of the era.

––––––––––

Most Americans, including most American lawyers, have an idealized and romanticized perception of Theodore Roosevelt, as one of our most influential leaders and one of the four faces on Mount Rushmore.

In fact, he was an amazingly compelling and successful person, justifiably recognized as one of America's greatest heroes, whose forceful personality and dramatic achievements still captivate biographers and readers of history, almost one hundred years after his death.

But he was also something more than his noteworthy achievements, someone whose full life story is deeply troubling, yet instructive to the legal profession. At no time during his exciting life did he ever truly embrace the rule of law. And the older he got, and the more burned out his sensibilities, the more his manic and self-righteous personality turned toward the dark side, and the less he respected our American legal system. In the end, "the wonderful little machine," who Henry James once greatly admired in his younger days, crashed and burned in infamy.

Theodore Roosevelt's life had a rise and a fall, both equally dramatic. To explain where he, the biographer, came out "in the end" on the subject of his magnificent trilogy, as well as where he puts Roosevelt's story in the historical understanding of the human condition, Morris relies on wisdom articulated in 1781 by the great Samuel Johnson, in his book *The Lives of the Poets*, which Morris uses as the epigram for *Colonel Roosevelt*:

> It has been observed in all ages, that the advantages of
> nature or of fortune have contributed very little to the

promotion of happiness; and that those whom the splendour of their rank, or the extent of their capacity, have placed upon the summits of human life, have not often given any just occasion to envy in those who look to them from a lower station; whether it be that apparent superiority incites great designs, and great designs are naturally liable to fatal miscarriages; or that the general lot of mankind is misery, and the misfortunes of those, whose eminence drew upon them an universal attention, have been more carefully recorded, because they were more generally observed, and have in reality been only more conspicuous than those of others, not more frequent, or more severe.

CHAPTER FIVE

Achieving Dispute Resolution: The Lawyer's End Game

After his speech at the 2000 Dallas Bar Association Bench Bar Conference, keynote speaker Jan Schlichtmann, attorney for the citizens of Woburn, Massachusetts, in their marathon toxic tort litigation battle profiled in the book *A Civil Action*, was asked what he considered to be his biggest mistake in the handling of the lawsuit. He answered without hesitation, "I faced each critical juncture in the case as a warrior and not as a problem solver."

Mr. Schlichtmann's comment on the pitfalls of the warrior's mind-set in litigation brought to mind an observation on the topic of war made by Dwight Eisenhower over fifty years ago: "I hate war as only a soldier who has lived it can, only as one who has seen its brutality, its stupidity."[1]

The connection between litigation and war first became apparent to me almost twenty years ago. In the course of my deposing an

---

Facing page: Lavaca County Courthouse jury box. Photo courtesy of Geoff Winningham.

1. Dwight D. Eisenhower, address before the Canadian Club, Ottawa, Canada, January 10, 1946, accessed September 7, 2011, http://www.eisenhower.archives.gov/all_about_ike/quotes.html.

expert witness, things got rather animated when the man under oath testified to a series of absurdly unfounded conclusions. My disgust with the witness grew as his baseless testimony continued, causing me to question him with a more aggressive attitude as the afternoon went on. A few days later, the expert confided to a mutual friend that he found it hard to believe I could purport to be a Christian in the context of the rough treatment he had received from my rather vicious examination of him.

Not long after the deposition ended, the case settled. Since the expert and I apparently traveled in the same social circles, to minimize any hard feelings, I took him to breakfast and learned he had never before testified in a lawsuit, which made his negative reaction to the examination experience more understandable. I asked him if he remembered the scene early in the movie *Butch Cassidy and the Sundance Kid*, where Paul Newman confronted a gang led by a mammoth actor. As they prepared for an imminent knife fight, Newman announced that they first needed to go over the rules.

The villain, on the verge of striking Newman with the first blow, became suddenly confused, stopped his thrust, and bellowed, "Rules? In a knife fight? No rules!" Just as the giant finished his remark, the ever-wily Butch Cassidy whacked his oversized opponent below the belt, knocked him out, and retreated to safety.

"If you understand what happened in that scene," I told the witness, "then you can understand what the cross-examination of an adverse witness in a lawsuit is all about. There is no Emily Post code of etiquette. It's a knife fight, and there ain't no rules."

The comparison between litigation and war goes beyond the hand-to-hand combat of cross-examination. The typical two-year path from the time a lawsuit is filed until it goes to trial is a battlefield riddled with landmines. These hidden explosives can take the form of witnesses with selective memories, documents full of ambiguous language, unanticipated massive expense, suddenly insolvent defendants, and certain judges calling shots in unjustified ways because of a politically cozy relationship with opposing counsel. With these dangers ever present, a party traversing the litigation minefield with even the best lawyer can find himself a target in the equivalent of guerrilla warfare.

All experienced trial lawyers, including Jan Schlichtmann, know this and also realize that in a world changing at the speed of light, where time is often more valuable than money, the prudent client's goal for his existing dispute is not to survive as the battle-scarred victor at the conclusion of a multiyear war of attrition, but rather is to achieve a prompt and acceptable resolution through creative tactics calculated to produce an expedited satisfactory result long before he has to face a jury.

Wait a second! Hasn't the prospect of facing a jury to end one's conflicts always been viewed as desirable in the United States of America? Sometimes yes; sometimes no. Veteran mediator Harlan Martin, once an esteemed judge in Dallas who presided over a few hundred jury trials in a prior life, has often told me that he starts his mediations with a thought few lawyers and even fewer parties would likely have reached on their own. Explaining at the outset why that day's mediation is the best day for concluding the dispute at hand, Harlan comments, "If we don't get this lawsuit settled today, then you'll get to go try this case and put your fate in the hands of twelve people who aren't smart enough to get off of jury duty." Most respond to this bit of unexpected insight from a former trial judge with a brief, tight smile. Then after a few seconds, Harlan's truth starts to sink in.

As guaranteed by the Constitution's Bill of Rights, citizens in our country have a constitutional right to trial by jury. This phenomenon has produced a dramatic history of parties and lawyers putting their fate in the hands of nonprofessional fact finders, euphemistically called a "jury of one's peers," which (like most things in life) has advantages and disadvantages, such as the following:

- Plaintiffs' lawyers favor jury trials because they provide the highest likelihood of awarding large actual and punitive damage awards. Defense lawyers favor them when a trial judge has underwhelming horsepower, well-known biases, and/or unpredictable judgment, and the odds of success favor going with twelve heads over one.

- Who shows up on a jury panel, who gets challenged off a panel, and who gets picked to serve on the jury affects the trial's outcome and therefore adds to its uncertainty.

- Jury questions and instructions often involve unfamiliar words and seemingly foreign syntax, which brings the element of unintelligibility into the deliberation process, adding to the uncertainty of a trial's conclusion.

- With a captive audience of novice fact finders in place, litigators usually engage in more theatrics and gamesmanship in front of juries, which causes the roller-coaster ride of a trial to have higher highs and lower lows.

- Studies of the jury system have proved that jurors often make up their minds about a trial's outcome by the end of the trial lawyers' opening statements, meaning final decisions get reached before the first witness gets called—totally contrary to the way a fact finder is instructed to do his job.

- Jury trials necessarily last longer than nonjury trials, typically take longer to get reached on a court's docket, and can result in a mistrial, making them more costly than bench trials.

WHY THERE ARE FEWER TRIALS

Over time, recognizing these realities of jury trials, problem-solving lawyers with egos not consumed by a warrior's mentality have learned to utilize two dispute-resolution tools that result in fewer cases getting disposed of by juries. These same tools have also produced fewer bench trials.

DISCOVERY HAS INCREASED THE LIKELIHOOD OF SETTLEMENT

Lawsuits often get settled because of thorough, well-executed discovery, which provides parties and their lawyers with a more in-formed basis for predicting their case's likely outcome. It removes many clouds from a party's crystal ball, and if the future can be determined now, then why keep paying expensive lawyers to march toward an inevitable result?

In his September 1980 lectures at Baylor Law School, since compiled in book form in *The Lawyer in Society*, Leon Jaworski addressed how increased discovery has affected the litigation process:

> There are endless . . . opportunities for the taking of depositions and obtaining evidence in advance, to know pretty well what the facts are at the time of trial. I think it takes the sport out of the trial to a large degree, but we just can't help that; we're still seeking justice. I think that, today, with all the advancements that have been made in pre-trial discovery, I think that the jousting, the sport of combat, in the courtroom, has been lessened to some degree. But we should not mourn that; we should praise that, really.[2]

Discovery in Texas state courts, however, used to be a deeply flawed process, allowing unscrupulous attorneys to frustrate any effort to nail down a case's facts. Fortunately, many of those flaws became greatly diminished in 1999 by some esteemed judges and lawyers who led the movement to change the discovery rules, thereby ending most of the obfuscatory games that had been played too long by too many. This successful effort in allowing discovery to achieve its intended purpose of finding all sides of truth in a case is a clear example of top professionals "raising the bar" to enhance our system of legal justice, as I explained in a 1999 *Dallas Morning News* editorial, reprinted below.[3]

Texas Finally Fixes a Broken Discovery Process

Anyone suffering the misfortune of being involved in litigation in Texas knows that the battle usually doesn't get won in the courtroom. Nearly 95 percent of all lawsuits filed get settled before being called to trial.

---

2. Leon Jaworski, *The Lawyer in Society* (Waco, TX: Baylor University Press, 2007), 36.

3. Talmage Boston, "Face Lift: Texas Finally Fixes a Broken 'Discovery Process,'" *Dallas Morning News*, January 10, 1999. Reprinted with permission of the *Dallas Morning News*.

Far removed from the dramatic uncertainty of facing a jury, dispute resolution typically hinges on the outcome of depositions in an office conference room, document production in a storage warehouse, and investigation of a computer's hard drive, which more often than not preserves deleted e-mail. This pretrial process where lawyers investigate the facts in a case is called "discovery."

Thanks to the efforts of some of Texas' top judges and lawyers, led by Supreme Court Justice Nathan Hecht and attorneys Steve Susman (from Houston) and Luke Soules (from San Antonio), pretrial discovery in Texas has just gotten a much-needed face lift with rules that became effective Jan 1. The impact on the process should be anything but cosmetic.

Those of us involved in Texas litigation during the past 20 years knew that the discovery process was "broken" and couldn't be salvaged by simply a quick fix.

What was broken? For one thing, the deposition process. In the movie *Butch Cassidy and the Sundance Kid*, after being disabled from a surprise blow below the belt, bad guy Ted Cassidy learns too late, "There's no rules in a knife fight." Until now, there have been essentially no hard and fast rules in a deposition.

Before this year, one lawyer would ask a key question of an adversarial witness. In an unfortunately recurring scenario, before the witness could respond, either (1) his attorney would spew out a rambling objection calculated to coach him or (2) he and his counsel would caucus privately so that he could be told how to answer.

Beyond the shameless witness-coaching game, another frequent abuse of the deposition process was its seemingly unlimited nature. Sometimes, a deposition that should take just two hours would last two days or longer. Also, lawyers in a case involving just three knowledgeable people were known to take the depositions of anyone even remotely involved in the dispute.

This pattern too often produced the phenomenon of

litigation extortion. A party's lawyer—carefully selected on the basis of his take-no-prisoners reputation—would call the opposing counsel and spell out his discovery game plan ("I will be taking the depositions of witnesses A through Z . . ."), which obviously would be wildly time-consuming and, therefore, wildly expensive. In cases involving a claim for less than $250,000, a defendant probably was better off financially to settle for an amount less than the anticipated cost of his defense, even when he had done nothing wrong.

The new discovery rules in Texas address such deposition evils. No more rambling coaching objections. No more post-question, pre-answer private caucus conferences except to discuss the application of a privilege. No depositions longer than six hours. No capacity to blackmail by threatening to take scores of depositions because, absent a court order, the number of deposition hours now spent in a case is limited.

Another "broken" part of the discovery process before this year involved written interrogatories and the production of documents. As just one example of the problem, too much time (and, therefore, too much money) was spent asking boilerplate questions. There also was no capacity to obtain documents from nonparty witnesses without the formality (and expense) of taking the witnesses' depositions.

The 1999 Texas discovery rule changes fix those problems, too. A simple new pleading called a "request for disclosure" eliminates the need for preparing boilerplate interrogatories. And a nonparty now can be subpoenaed to produce documents without the need for a deposition.

Finally, in our increasingly paperless world where much communication is in the form of e-mail and where many company records are kept on a computer system, the new rules provide procedures for the retrieval of electronic or magnetic data.

Dan Jenkins once said, "Ain't nuthin' in life is dead

solid perfect." Certainly, that will prove true of the 1999 discovery rule changes. But Texans should take comfort in knowing that their judges and lawyers recognized the serious problems that have existed in the discovery phases of the lawsuit business and attempted to address them in a way that benefits all who find themselves entwined in the agonizing, expensive, and unpredictable process of dispute resolution. Better late than never.

MEDIATION AND ARBITRATION HAVE CAUSED FEWER TRIALS

After discovery is essentially completed, mediation usually follows. In the last two decades, most judges won't try a case unless it's been mediated to the point of impasse. A hardball "agent of reality" mediator helps remove most of the crystal ball's few remaining clouds after the discovery closes. Across the board, approximately three-fourths of the cases that get mediated result in settlement. If our system had fewer mediations, more cases would definitely get tried.

In the realm of alternative dispute resolution, besides the rise in settlements caused by the increased use of mediation, in recent years, more and more commercial contracts contain arbitration provisions. The business community (rightly or wrongly) perceives arbitration to be advantageous to litigation because (1) there is a fear of runaway juries; (2) an arbitrator's expertise in the subject of the dispute often exceeds that of trial judges; (3) it is binding, and therefore a final resolution after an arbitration will result in prompt closure and will not be delayed by appeal and possible retrial; (4) arbitration settings are more likely than trial dates to go on the day scheduled (thereby avoiding the problem of trial resettings, which cause additional lawyer preparation time and therefore additional expense); (5) arbitration typically has less discovery and thus less likelihood for discovery abuse; (6) arbitration is perceived as less costly than litigation due to all the circumstances described above (even though the parties have to pay arbitrators a fee, while judges' salaries are paid by taxpayers); and (7) confidentiality exists in the arbitration process, meaning any dirty laundry in a case won't get aired out in a public courtroom.

In *The Lawyer in Society*, Leon Jaworski predicted the rise of arbitration as a favored resolution tool:

> If we don't find a way of avoiding the high cost of litigation and the delays in litigation, you're going to see more and more arbitration. There's no need in guessing about it. It's a foregone conclusion that it will happen. Arbitration is beginning to be thought of, and I think will become more significant; it will be resorted to more often than in the past and there'll be new vehicles set up in order to avoid the high cost of litigation and the long delays.[4]

With the statistical reduction in jury trials and bench trials due to the effects of more effective discovery and the increased use of mediation and arbitration, the ultimate question arises: Is the national decline in civil trials throughout the United States a good thing or a bad thing? My response came in my *Dallas Business Journal* column from a few years ago, reprinted below, when the reality of the vanishing trial first became apparent.[5]

Fewer Civil Trials: Good or Bad?

Addressing a State Bar of Texas Litigation Section seminar two months ago, Fifth Circuit Judge Patrick Higginbotham gave his highly informed and respected opinion on the topic that seems to consume the litigation community these days: "The vanishing civil trial."

Judge Higginbotham provided facts to prove what litigators already know—the days of congested dockets in big cities are gone because so few cases go to trial these days.

Statistics tell the tale. The percentage of jury and bench trials in federal civil cases across the country has declined from 10% of cases resolved in 1970 to 2.2% in 2001. Juries resolved 4.3% of federal civil cases in 1970 and

---

4. Jaworski, *The Lawyer in Society*, 81.

5. Talmage Boston, "Fewer Civil Trials: Good or Bad?" *Dallas Business Journal*, April 2, 2004. Reprinted with permission of the *Dallas Business Journal*.

only 1.5%—3,633 cases in raw numbers—in 2001.

Judge Higginbotham essentially blamed alternative dispute resolution as the cause of trials' declining numbers, and then expressed his concern that too many settlements arising out of mediations harms our legal system because it reduces the amount of court-created precedent that serves as the basis for our common law.

No one can dispute that more settlements mean fewer trials, which in turn mean fewer appeals, which in turn means less precedent. A district judge in Dallas typically tries only 13 to 15 jury trials per year, since the county courts at law acquired concurrent jurisdiction more than six years ago. Most of those cases involve either car wrecks, grocery store slip-and-falls, or terminated employees who have no written employment agreements.

Thus, those few lawsuits that go to trial almost always involve plaintiffs who have their lawyer hired on a contingent-fee basis, such that they essentially have no downside to rolling the dice at trial since it does not cost them any money to proceed.

One Dallas district judge told me in early February that the judge had not had a jury trial go past voir dire since the first week in November. A justice on the Dallas Court of Appeals confirmed the impact on appellate practice, telling me in late January that it had been over two months since the justice last heard an oral argument.

The ultimate question for all people having any interest in the American system of jurisprudence now becomes: "Is the vanishing civil trial a good thing or a bad thing?"

Maybe the question deserves some tweaking: "A good thing or a bad thing for whom?" Therein lies the rub.

Certainly, trials are good things for those of us, litigators and judges, who spend our careers involved in the business of lawsuits. Historically, they are what we most enjoy doing in our practice, and where reputations are made. Until recently, trials have been what notched our belts.

In over a quarter of a century practicing as a trial lawyer in downtown Dallas, however, I have yet to have a client who truly wanted to proceed through the entire litigation process of going to trial and then proceeding through an appeal when an acceptable settlement became available. I have always represented business people. They don't like paying enormous, out-of-pocket fees. Most important, they prefer to decide their own fate in bringing closure to a dispute, over having closure brought by some combination of a jury, a politically elected or appointed trial judge, or an appellate court.

I respectfully disagree with Judge Higginbotham as to the cause of the vanishing civil trial.

In my opinion, it is not caused so much by the influx and effect of alternative dispute resolutions; rather it is a natural result of the development of discovery over the last few decades. Improved discovery, as applied by veteran practitioners, removed the possibility of trial by ambush, and allowed parties assisted by competent counsel to evaluate the pertinent facts in a case in advance of trial. It also handicaps their likelihood for success in the trial, and causes them to evaluate how much pursuing and appealing a trial will cost them, analyze the solvency of a defendant, and arrive at a reasonable settlement.

John Ashcroft is not everyone's favorite lawyer. But his remarks to the University of Missouri-Columbia Law School graduation ceremony in the spring of 2002 tie all these points together.

The Attorney General explained to the law students how and why our legal system works today in the disposition of civil disputes, saying, "Justice can be achieved through consensus as well as litigation. Adversarial and consensus justice are mutually reinforcing concepts; behind every successful mediation of a dispute is the prospect of aggressive litigation. And behind all successful litigation must be the opportunity for citizens to work together to reach a mutually beneficial outcome."

Let all the people say, "Amen."

———————————————

To my surprise, as I worked on writing this chapter, the Summer 2010 issue of the American Bar Association's *Litigation: The Journal of the Section of Litigation* arrived in the mail. In her "Opening Statement" column, then ABA Litigation Section Chair Hilarie Bass (with the Miami, Florida, office of the Greenberg Traurig law firm) had thoughts that essentially matched my own on the subject of dispute-resolution transformation in American jurisprudence over the last few years, and she expressed them persuasively.

Amazing! Before reading her ABA column, I had never met or had communication with Hilarie Bass. She's performed her litigation business in another part of the country with different clients appearing before different tribunals for almost as long as I have. Yet despite these dissimilarities between us, we've arrived at the same place at the same time on how we view the changes in the field of dispute resolution over the course of our respective careers. To quote best-selling author Spencer Johnson, "the cheese has moved" in the dispute-resolution arena, and prudent lawyers all over the country had better move with it, instead of waxing eloquent in sorrow over the diminishing role of the civil trial in our legal system.

With Hilarie's and the ABA's permission, her well-considered column appears below.[6]

———————————————

The End of the Justice System as We Knew It?

Much has been said about recent statistics that show that currently only about 1 percent of cases filed in our courts are actually resolved through trial. As the largest group of attorneys in the United States who profess to specialize in trial work, we are forced to consider the

———————————————

6. Hilarie Bass, "The End of the Justice System as We Knew It?," *Litigation* 36, no. 4 (Summer 2010): 1–2. © 2010 by the American Bar Association. Reprinted with permission. This information or any portion thereof may not be copied or disseminated in any form or by any means or stored in an electronic database or retrieval system without the express written consent of the American Bar Association.

broad implications for our profession, the justice system, and our clients.

Many of the court-imposed innovations over the last decades have certainly contributed to this result. The use of a rules system that requires that all facts will be known, all documents will be reviewed, and all witnesses will be interviewed well in advance of trial can make case presentation in court anticlimactic, predictable, and scripted. In addition, a process that mandates mediation before an objective third party, trained to convince the parties of the expense and uncertainty of a trial, weighs heavily on clients to seriously consider resolving their dispute before trial. And, of course, the enormous expense of a trial seems much harder to justify when even the most able of trial lawyers find it difficult to predict the outcome.

Rather than lamenting the scarcity of trials, litigators must first evaluate whether this decline suggests an erosion of our justice system or is simply the inevitable result of a number of strategies imposed by courts and lawyers alike to expedite and economize the cost of dispute resolution. Our history reflects the significant impact that trials have had on leading us through important social change. Landmark cases are the heart and soul of our judiciary, and the significance that the resolution of such social issues represents to the advancement of our society cannot be overestimated. Is it necessarily a bad thing that garden-variety commercial disputes are typically resolved before trial?

In answering this question, most would agree that there are certain rationales for pretrial settlement that are unacceptable. If parties wish to have their dispute resolved by trial but believe the expense will be too great, this is a problem we must address. Additionally, if potential litigants perceive that holding out for a trial will cause an unacceptable delay in the resolution of their dispute, then we must repair the effectiveness of our judicial system. Similarly, result-oriented judging, where judges leave critical legal issues unresolved until just prior to trial in the hope that uncertainty will force the parties to settle, should also be viewed as intolerable.

We must determine the percentage of cases that are settled pretrial for the above reasons before we can remedy the problem of the disappearing jury trial. While all litigants' behavior is affected by the expense of the process, many of the parties with the most at stake are likely not evaluating whether or not to take a case to trial on that basis alone. Many clients choose settlement because the discovery process provides sufficient information to evaluate the merits of their claims and defenses. Once that is accomplished, the entry of a certain settlement based on a predicted result is often much more palatable than the uncertainty of the jury process. The complexity of common factual issues likely to come before an unsophisticated venire is often enough to instill fear in the hearts of litigants. Add to that the inherent biases of many jurors against corporate litigants in general, and certain industry groups in particular, and you have a scenario where many litigants make a well-reasoned, rational decision to resolve their dispute by entry of a voluntary pretrial agreement.

If the decision to settle pretrial is not a result of a broken system but more a statement about the complexities of many disputes and the inherent challenges they pose for our system, perhaps it is instead time to focus on the long-term effect of this new reality on our justice system. As trial lawyers, we are often disappointed by a client's decision to settle. Is it irrational for that evaluation to take precedence over our desire to see who wins and who loses at trial?

Few among us have not questioned how to best train our young lawyers given that many of them will not get the opportunity to try a case for years after being admitted to practice. In our effort to develop new training methods to assist our young lawyers in becoming effective advocates, we must place greater emphasis on areas of expertise required by the justice system in which they will operate—with greater emphasis on mediation; counseling of clients; and all forms of alternative dispute resolution, from summary jury trials to non-binding arbitration.

Believing that there is only a minimal chance of resolving a dispute in a trial setting substantially affects the way we prepare our cases. Our traditional strategies of holding the best for cross-examination at trial and reserving issues for experts so as not to afford a dress rehearsal for the trial obviously fall by the wayside when going to trial is unlikely. Pretrial often is the only opportunity to inform the opposition and other interested parties of the strength of our case and the relative weakness of theirs. Similar modifications to the nature and extent of discovery are an inevitable result of prosecuting a matter with the recognition that the case is unlikely to be tried to conclusion.

Offering rule changes that will improve the process will certainly assist our clients and create greater efficiency. In the end, however, the uncertainty of hoping that six or 12 jurors can be appropriately informed about the factual complexities of a sophisticated commercial dispute—and objective enough to divorce themselves from their implicit biases and inherent prejudices—is more likely to compel litigants to choose the certainty of a self-directed settlement than all the rule changes we can write. Perhaps our focus going forward should be on helping our clients resolve their disputes in the most expeditious and economic way—regardless of whether or not the result is a trial.

ONE REMAINING UNSOLVED PROBLEM: PARTISAN POLITICAL JUDICIAL ELECTIONS

Despite the dispute-resolution transformation that's taken place in recent decades, one fundamental flaw still exists to the detriment of all involved in our system of civil justice, and it further militates in favor of a lawyer's getting his client's dispute resolved sooner rather than later to avoid the vagaries of a trial. That most notable flaw is the fact that in Texas (and thirty-seven other states), citizens elect trial and appellate judges in partisan political elections.

In rural, less populous counties, residents are in a position to actually know or at least have some idea about the performance of their single district judge who presides over the lone courtroom in their county courthouse, such that when they cast their vote for judge in his election or reelection year, they are usually making an informed decision.

In an increasingly urbanized state, however, where the substantial majority of the people live in and around large cities, in recent years, voters have had to face a ballot filled with dozens of judicial elections, listing the names of strangers as candidates for civil district courts, criminal district courts, family district courts, probate courts, county courts at law, justice of the peace courts, courts of appeal, the criminal court of appeal, and the supreme court. Even the lawyer who spends his career trying cases and arguing motions before some of these judges has no personal knowledge about the job performance of the other candidates who are either on or seeking to take the bench in courts outside that attorney's practice area. Our nonlawyer friends invariably contact us shortly before election day and ask the same question: "Which judges should I vote for?" Our best answer is usually, "I don't know most of them myself. I can tell you who the good civil judges are, but for the rest of the races, it's usually safe to vote for who our local newspaper endorses."

In summary, our current system of selecting judges in partisan political elections, particularly in cities where there are several dozen contested races on each ballot, is a total breakage in our legal system that no one has succeeded in fixing and provides a fundamentally absurd method for determining how justice in our state should be administered. I addressed this ill-considered aspect of partisan

judicial elections in a 2010 column for the *Dallas Business Journal,*
reprinted below.[7]

The Insane Reality of Partisan Judicial Elections

A caveat on the front end. All current and past local
judges can rest easy—no name is mentioned in this column. Any judges who believe these comments are aimed
at them are drawing their own conclusions.

On the morning of Nov. 2, 2010, I went to our neigh-
borhood grade school to vote. In reviewing the front and
back of the ballot, I had two options—I could either
black out one oval (and thereby vote a straight ticket for
one party) and be finished voting in 15 seconds; or else I
could black out more than 100 ovals by making a selection in each race on the ballot, a process that would take
at least 3 minutes.

Although most of my choices were for the candidates of one party, some were for the judicial candidates
aligned with the other party, whom I knew from firsthand
experience as a practicing trial lawyer were doing a good
job at presiding over the cases assigned to their courts.
In good conscience, therefore, I had only one real voting
option—and it was the 3-minute process.

Obviously, most Dallas County residents are not trial
lawyers. This substantial majority of our local population,
therefore, very rarely has occasion to visit a courtroom
and see a trial judge in action.

Like every other line of work, some judges are good
(i.e., fair, smart, diligent, responsible, emotionally intelligent, efficient, etc.); some are average; and some are bad
and should not be on the bench.

When the nontrial lawyer goes to vote and sees several
dozen contested judicial races on the ballot, he almost
always has no personal knowledge of whether the person

---

7. Talmage Boston, "The Insane Reality of Partisan Judicial Elections," *Dallas Business Journal,*
November 19, 2010. Reprinted with permission of the *Dallas Business Journal.*

getting his vote is a good, average, or bad judge.

The only thing the voter knows about the judicial candidate is the black oval recipient's political party. That being the case, if a voter feels aligned with one party, and has no reliable means of determining who the good and bad judges are, then why not pick the 15-second option on Election Day, and vote the straight party line?

Having been a practicing trial lawyer in Dallas for more than 32 years, I have seen eras when local judges were all Republican and times when they were all Democrat. We have had great judges and weak judges from both parties preside over local courtrooms for extended periods of time.

Personally, I have no preference for Republican or Democratic judges. I only have a preference for judges who are fair, smart, diligent, responsible, emotionally intelligent, and efficient.

With surging population growth throughout the state (and particularly in North Texas) predicted to continue, the number of courts needed to handle civil, family, and criminal trials will surely increase. That means ballots in future elections will list even more contested judicial races than now, making it more impossible to know whether the judges getting votes perform their duties well, average, or poorly.

At the very least, the current uninformed process of electing judges in Texas should be modified to where the person who chooses the 15-second voting process on Election Day is voting only for executive and legislative candidates of her chosen political party. The only intelligent way to vote for judges should be on a court-by-court basis, with there being no judicial candidate whose political party affiliation is disclosed on the ballot.

In each contested race, on my proposed ballot for future elections, the voter would have the following three choices for filling in his chosen oval:

District Court, Dallas County, Texas

- ○ John Doe
- ○ Mary Snow
- ○ No Knowledge or Opinion

In addition to the current scenario whereby judges get selected solely because of their party affiliation, the second main flaw in our current method of choosing which candidates shall preside over our trial and appellate courts is that the political process essentially builds incentives into the judicial system for recurrent bribery.

How so?

Pertinent fact #1: To get elected judge in a large city in the last twenty years routinely has necessitated a candidate's raising hundreds of thousands of dollars to fund his campaign's publicity efforts.

Pertinent fact #2: In contested judicial races, the main financial supporters of the judicial candidates are lawyers, law firms, and parties to lawsuits.

Rhetorical question: Who is more likely to get a favorable ruling from a judge—the lawyer representing one party who has made a substantial donation to the judge's campaign or the lawyer representing the other party who has made no donation to the judge's war chest (or, heaven forbid, has made a donation to the judge's opponent in the last election)?

I addressed the reality of bribery inherent in a system where judges get elected in expensive partisan political elections in a 2000 *Dallas Morning News* column, reprinted below.[8]

Filmmaker Would Have a Field Day with State's System of Electing Judges

It occasionally takes the artistry of a filmmaker to awaken the multitudes to the necessity of reforming a broken system. For any budding Spielberg aspiring to rake

---

8. Talmage Boston, "Texas Justice: Filmmaker Would Have a Field Day with State's System of Electing Judges," *Dallas Morning News*, July 9, 2000. Reprinted with permission of the *Dallas Morning News*.

a little muck, our Texas system of electing state judges is out there, just waiting for the cameras to roll.

The film's introduction, narrated by Atticus Finch/ Gregory Peck, would advise the viewer that the scenes depicted don't reflect most of our state's judges, who actually are diligent, fair-minded, intelligent, and public-spirited. But the film would show certain events that have occurred in the recent past and reflect the evils of the status quo.

The documentary's first scene would take place at the traditional campaign fundraiser, set at either a swanky private club on the top floor of a skyscraper or the mansion of some rich lawyer. Endless varieties of hors d'oeuvres fill the tables. Booze flows. White-coated servants tend to guests' needs. And in the center of the crowd, nuzzling next to the candidate, are the underwriting hosts, each smoothly ensuring that the event accomplishes its two purposes—to expand the judge's political war chest and to endear the hosts to their guest of honor so as to build up a reserve of good will, readily accessible for the next close legal call at a hearing or trial.

Cut. Move to the courthouse office of the incumbent judge running for re-election. A contested hearing has just concluded, the judge has taken the matter under advisement, and it now is time for the squeeze. A messenger discretely summons one of the lawyers (still anxious and uncertain about the hearing's outcome) to the judge's chambers. In words carefully chosen, with all doors closed, the candidate raises an eyebrow and subtly expresses how much he or she would appreciate it if the attorney could get his law firm to jump on the campaign bandwagon with endorsements and money.

Cut. The next scene takes place in the courtroom shortly after election day. The judge has been defeated. He or she remembers the lawyers who supported the successful adversary, and one of those lawyers now has come to argue his case. An unexpected ruling results, seemingly at odds with the law and the facts and to the detriment of the attorney who supported the victorious candidate. The rationale behind the decision seems pure retaliation.

The lawyer on the short end of the ruling promptly files a motion to recuse. Amazingly, the judge ignores the well-established procedure for responding to such a challenge and refuses to either withdraw from the case or refer the motion to the presiding administrative judge. A mandamus to the court of appeals straightens out the situation but at significant expense and aggravation to the unfortunate client whose lawyer misplayed his politics.

Those are just a few of the scenes in the documentary that probably never will get made about the pitfalls of electing judges in Texas.

The problem is this: Politicians are expected to have an agenda and be partial. That is what voters are supporting when they contribute campaign funding and elect their chosen candidate. Judges, on the other hand, are required to be impartial. When litigants come before them, the arbiter is supposed to evaluate only the equities (and not the politics) of the parties involved in a particular dispute.

In a system where theoretically impartial judges are required to become politicians in order to get elected, the inherent conflict sometimes causes the black-robed vehicle to veer off the road into the partisan politics ditch.

There are other, more satisfactory alternatives for judicial selection, most notably the Missouri Plan, where judges are appointed and confirmed by blue-ribbon panels and state government leaders and then, after serving a few years, simply run against their record in an election. If the voter thinks the judge has been fair, hard-working, and smart, he votes "yes." If his honor's performance has been unsatisfactory, the elector votes "no." If the judge loses the election against his own record, a successor is appointed.

Certainly, Texas has its fair share of strong state court

judges who resist political pressures, maintain their impartiality, and do a fine job of dispersing justice. Nonetheless, under our current system of electing judges, the client seeking to maximize his position in a dispute should be aware of an emerging and troubling axiom in the profession: "The good lawyer knows the law. The great lawyer knows the judge."

CONCLUSION

Taking into consideration the issues addressed in this chapter, those lawyers aspiring to elevate both our profession and our system of jurisprudence must be ever vigilant and ever creative in finding ways to achieve prompt resolution of their clients' disputes. Trials and appeals should be the final option available to dispose of a conflict, and it should disturb no one who understands the way things work in our civil justice system that successful parties guided by prudent lawyers position themselves in ways that avoid the anxiety, expense, uncertainty, and sometimes the injustice that comes with pursuing that final option.

As one biographer, Brian Dirck, concluded, esteemed litigator Abraham Lincoln saw that his primary role as a lawyer was to aspire to serve as the "grease" that lubricates the machinery of society and thereby allow people to function at their most efficient and productive levels. As you will recall from chapter 1, Lincoln advised young lawyers in his community thusly:

> Discourage litigation. Persuade your neighbors to compromise whenever you can. Point out to them how the nominal winner is often a real loser—in fees, expenses, and waste of time. As a peacemaker the lawyer has a superior opportunity of being a good man. There will still be business enough.[9]

---

9. Abraham Lincoln's Notes for a Law Lecture, accessed September 22, 2011, http://showcase.netins.net/web/creative/lincoln/speeches/lawlect.htm.

Knowing his perspective on the wisdom in achieving prompt dispute resolution, if Honest Abe Lincoln somehow reappeared in twenty-first century America and learned that his beloved constitutional system of civil justice had entered the era of the "vanishing trial," I suspect he would be as delighted with that circumstance as he would be to learn that in 2008 the citizens of his country had elected an African American to serve as president of the United States.

Acknowledgments

This book would never have materialized without the support of the State Bar of Texas's leaders and personnel, for whom I've had the privilege of serving in a variety of capacities. Past SBOT presidents Kelly Frels, Eduardo Rodriguez, Martha Dickie, Gib Walton, Harper Estes, Roland Johnson, and Terry Tottenham and current president Bob Black have all been sources of encouragement and support through the years; as have past Litigation Council chairs Doak Bishop, Kim Askew, John Simpson, Luke Soules, Andy Tindel, Dan Bishop, Susan Nelson, Alistair Dawson, Elizabeth Mack, Fred Bowers, and Walker Friedman and current chair Linda McDonald; as have the members of the SBOT's incredible staff with whom I've worked most closely—Executive Director Michelle Hunter and her stellar team of Kelley Jones King, Pat Nester, Sharon Sandle, Tracy Nuckols, Courtney Cavaliere, and Lara Talkington, as well as former employees Kevin Priestner and Holly Wilkerson Priestner. Through these colleagues, over the last fourteen years, the SBOT has nurtured and enhanced my commitment and contribution to the profession.

This book also came to fruition because of the support of certain key people at Winstead PC, the law firm where I've worked since 1997—Kevin Sullivan, Jay Madrid, Wayne Bost, John Nolan, Mike Alessio, Michelle Rieger, David Dawson, Keith Mullen, Roland Love, Jeff Hage, and Denis Braham.

Specific contributions to the book were made by former United States Attorney General Dick Thornburgh (who wrote the magnificent foreword and provided support for my focus on Atticus Finch); historian Ronald C. White Jr. (who blessed the accuracy of my overview of Abraham Lincoln's career in chapter 1 and provided other valuable editorial suggestions); Secretary James A. Baker, III (who allowed me to interview him for chapter 2 and gave me a wonderful endorsement on the dust jacket); Secretary Baker's assistant, John Williams (who gave me editorial suggestions for chapter 2); Gibson Gayle (longtime law partner and close friend of Leon Jaworski, who allowed me to interview him for chapter 2 and fact-checked the Jaworski part of that chapter as well); Richard Ben-Veniste (who reviewed my work in that part of chapter 2 devoted to Watergate); lawyer-novelists Richard North Patterson and John Grisham (who reviewed and affirmed my write-ups on them in chapter 3; Patterson also gave me a wonderful endorsement on the dust jacket); historians Douglas Brinkley, Doris Kearns Goodwin, and Edmund Morris (who each reviewed my assessment of Theodore Roosevelt in chapter 4); Jeffrey Toobin, Ken Starr, and Texas Supreme Court Chief Justice Wallace Jefferson (who each reviewed the book and blessed it with their endorsements on the dust jacket); former SBOT Litigation Section chairs Walker Friedman and Alistair Dawson (who gave me editorial suggestions for chapter 5); Austin lawyer and lifelong friend Bill Parrish (who greatly enhanced my appreciation of Atticus Finch); and Winstead colleagues Tom Van Arsdel and Kristen Sherwin (who assisted during my interviews of Messrs. Baker, Gayle, and Patterson).

The most meaningful sacrifice made on my behalf during the time I needed to research, write, and edit this book was made by my incredibly patient and supportive wife, Claire, while son Scott and daughter Lindsey provided a steady stream of encouragement. My parents, Paul and Mary Jane Boston, pointed me in the direction of Abraham Lincoln and Atticus Finch at a young age and then later directed me into the wonderful world of Louis Auchincloss, thereby opening my eyes to the possibility that a person could be both a full-time lawyer and a professional writer. My best friend, Marvin Blum, has been there for me whenever I've needed him ever since our first day at the University of Texas Law School. Finally, through the years, my greatest mentors in the legal profession—Charles Boston, Austin McCloud, Robert B. Payne, Lee Vendig, and Walter M. Spradley—to whom I have dedicated this book, all provided direction at critical junctures in my path as a lawyer.

The author and the State Bar of Texas are grateful to the following publishers and authors for permission to reprint text selections in this work:

Excerpts from Crossroads, *chapter 2*:
Reprinted from *Crossroads* by Leon Jaworski, © 1981 by Leon Jaworski. Used by permission of Claire Draper.

Excerpts from After Fifteen Years, *chapter 2*:
Reprinted from *After Fifteen Years* by Leon Jaworski, © 1961 by Leon Jaworski. Used by permission of Claire Draper.

Excerpts from The Right and the Power, *chapter 2*:
Reprinted from *The Right and the Power* by Leon Jaworski, © 1976 by Leon Jaworski. Used by permission of Claire Draper.

Excerpt from RN: The Memoirs of Richard Nixon, *chapter 2*:
Reprinted from *The Memoirs of Richard Nixon—Volume 1* by Richard Nixon, © 1978, 1990 by The Estate of Richard M. Nixon. Used by permission of Grand Central Publishing. All rights reserved.

Excerpts from Work Hard, Study . . . and Keep Out of Politics!, *chapter 2*:
Reprinted from *Work Hard, Study . . . and Keep Out of Politics!* by James A. Baker, III, with Steve Fiffer, © 2006 by James A. Baker, III. Used by permission of G.P. Putnam's Sons, a division of Penguin Group (USA) Inc.

Excerpts from The Politics of Diplomacy, *chapter 2*:
Reprinted from *The Politics of Diplomacy* by James A. Baker, III, © 1995 by James A. Baker, III. Used by permission of G.P. Putnam's Sons, a division of Penguin Group (USA) Inc.

Excerpts from The Power Game: How Washington Works, *chapter 2*:
Reprinted from *The Power Game: How Washington Works* by Hedrick Smith, © 1988 by Hedrick Smith. Used by permission of Random House, Inc.

Excerpts from President Reagan: The Role of a Lifetime, *chapter 2*:

By Talmage Boston. Reprinted with permission of the *Dallas Morning News.*

The articles "Fewer Civil Trials: Good or Bad?" and "The Insane Reality of Partisan Judicial Elections," chapter 5:
By Talmage Boston. Reprinted with permission of *Dallas Business Journal.*

The article "The End of the Justice System as We Knew It?", chapter 5:
By Hilarie Bass. © 2010 by the American Bar Association. Reprinted with permission. This information or any portion thereof may not be copied or disseminated in any form or by any means or stored in an electronic database or retrieval system without the express written consent of the American Bar Association.